Confessions Of An Intergalactic Anthropologist

Confessions Of An Intergalactic Anthropologist

by
Marcia Schafer

Confessions Of An Intergalactic Anthropologist
by Marcia Schafer

First Edition published in 1999, Second printing, revised 2002.

Published by

PMB D22
1334 E. Chandler Blvd. #5
Phoenix, AZ 85048
Tel: 480.460.7807
Fax: 480.460.7809

SAN299-7592
Cover Design by Neal Berg Design
Interior Design by The Printed Page
Back Cover Photo by Yale Rachlin
The interior images used herein were obtained from IMSI's MasterClips® Premium Image Collection, 75 Rowland Way, Novato Ca. 94945, USA.

Publishers Cataloging in Publication
(Provided by Quality Books, Inc.)

Schafer, Marcia.
Confessions of an intergalactic anthropologist / Marcia Schafer. -- 2nd ed.
p. cm.
LCCN: 98-93955
ISBN: 0-9668620-2-3

1. Schafer, Marcia. 2. Parapsychology and anthropology. 3. Human-alien encounters. 4. Reincarnation. 5. Unidentified flying objects--Sightings and encounters. 6. Psychics--Biography. I. Title

BF1045.A65S34 1999 133.8
QBI98-1559

Printed in the USA.

Here's what people are saying about *Confessions of an Intergalactic Anthropologist*

Nexus Magazine
"There are some remarkable revelations in this book, all the more so seeing Schafer is a logical, rational, common-sense sort of person..."

Art Bell, *After Dark Magazine*
"She even goes into what these several ET races are like with detail maybe rivaled only by the US military in their manuals on extraterrestrials..."

Zecharia Sitchin, Author of the *Earth Chronicles*
"I appreciate the various references to me and my writings, and your acceptance of the key role that gold played in the events recorded in my Earth Chronicles. Best wishes for your book's success."

Jim Marrs, Bestselling Author of *Crossfire; Alien Agenda*
"Marcia Schafer takes the reader on her very own special trip to the heart of the universe. Prepare to enter graduate school."

Jeffrey Mishlove, Author, Host of PBS series *Thinking Allowed*
"You have shown the ability to be both visionary and practical simultaneously."

Neil Freer, Author of *Breaking the Godspell; God Games*
"Years of close encounter grad school of the 6th kind in the criteria vacuum and still smiling and funny. This well balanced young woman's middle name is Courage. A voice for those who share the experience but don't know how to matriculate themselves."

Command Sgt. Major Robert Dean, International UFO Lecturer and Investigator
"Probably the most important and incredible thing I can say about this book is, in my opinion, it's true. This is a book from an author whose time has come."

R. Leo Sprinkle, Ph.D., Author of *Soul Samples: Personal Explorations in Reincarnation and UFO Experiences*
"Marcia Schafer provides the reader with a fascinating account of her encounters during multidimensional travel. Her journal reveals a Higher Self of courage, curiosity and compassion; her 'confessions' provide intellectual and spiritual nourishment for us all."

Peter Gersten, Executive Director of Citizens Against UFO Secrecy (CAUS)
"It's gratifying to see another emergence from the last of our closets. Ms Schafer is a true heroine in coming forward and proclaiming, 'I have been and still am in contact with another form of intelligence.' "

Michael Lindemann, Futurist
"Marcia Schafer is among the most clear and grounded experiencers I've ever come across."

Victor Beasley, Ph.D., Author of *Intuition by Design*
"Marcia Schafer writes with compelling authority that derives from both worldly experience and direct perception of unseen realties. Such an intimate understanding of natural forces is a goal for all of us inhabiting human bodies."

Dr Joseph Puleo, coauthor Healing Codes for the Biological Apocalypse
"Confessions of an Intergalactic Anthropologist is a great work and a must read."

Dedication

Thanks be to the memories of antiquity,
to the light of the eternal flame,
and to the One who carries the holy name.

To Dylan Thomas, our secret as we go gentle into the night. I offer thanks and share this Earthly success in a most heavenly manner. Peace in your journeys.

To those who believed in me,
thank you for walking within the inner circles.

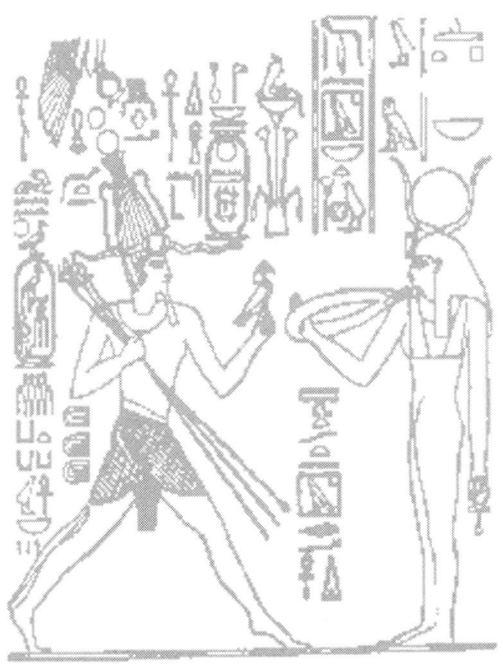

TABLE OF CONTENTS

Author's Notes

Every person must find his or her own version of truth

The contents of this book are intended to spur thought and realization about the nature of reality and the world in which we live. Although a concept may be presented in an authoritative manner, please do not accept it as valid if it does not feel right. It is important to question everything and apply only what fits with ease into your belief system. Remember, you are the sole navigator of your life in this human experience. To rely on someone else's version of truth is to relinquish responsibility to yourself. If I am able to assist with expanding your vision, I am honored.

Sometimes, when we receive information that is important to us, it is accompanied by signs that manifest physically within our body. Your higher consciousness will use these clues as a signal for you to pay attention. They may include:

- chills or a shiver up your spine ("shaman shivers")
- light flutters over your skin
- ringing in the ears, usually high pitched tones
- tingling of the extremities
- visual disturbances (flashes of light, blurring, spots)
- temporary disorientation

If you experience any of these physiological clues during the reading of this book, it may be a message for you to pay closer attention to the contents.

Editing the Channeled Messages

In some situations, the channeled passages were edited because the speaking style is sometimes a bit awkward, even ponderous, when transferred to writing. Some of the sources think differently than we do and hence have difficulty using our language. Picture a foreigner who uses inappropriate words and sentence structure. He may have interesting things to say, but it can be taxing for a listener to retrieve his message. Because of this, some of the passages required editing.

Many sentences started with "for" or "and," and most of these expressions have been removed. There are also areas where I added brief explanations in parentheses or as a footnote to help the reader better understand what is being talked about. Generally, most editing was done solely to improve grammar. I have tried to make sure that none of the messages were altered while preparing the text for publication.

Foreword

by Retired Command Sergeant Major Robert Dean

Retired Command Sergeant Major Robert Dean is a prominent UFO researcher and international lecturer who has spoken in over fourteen countries. While working for Supreme Headquarters Allied Powers Europe (SHAPE) in 1963, he had clearance to a highly classified, secret NATO report detailing government awareness of alien involvement with Earth. Mr. Dean has had numerous television and radio appearances and has been featured in countless publications.

Each of us is poised on the steps of a doorway into a frightening and infinite new reality—our old world is over and an uncertain future awaits us all. This new age, this new paradigm and a totally new form of life is evolving and is inevitable. We cannot run from it, we cannot hide from it and we cannot try to avoid it, because "it" is here and it is NOW.

Where we are going will take courage and strength. I suspect that many of us will not make the transition—many of us will falter. Some of us are not ready and all of us are a little bit afraid of this unknown. But Marcia Schafer is a brave and courageous young woman who has peeped through the doorway into another world and is willing to share with us what she has seen and what she has learned. She will help show us that we do not need to fear. Let us walk on knowing that there is hope, and with love and courage we will prevail. I for one commend her bravery and courage. I will look eagerly into our tomorrow with less fear. Now read on and don't be afraid.

INTRODUCTION

Why I Came Forward

Why Me?

I have been asked by some people, "Why do these things happen to you? Why not someone else?" The truth is that these things often do happen to others, only they won't always admit to it, at least in public. Only now, things are changing. People like me are coming forward by the hundreds.

Although others have made the claim of extraterrestrial contact, each of us brings a different facet to the phenomenon. We each describe what we have experienced with other life forms, thus providing slightly different perspectives about a common event. I am hopeful that those who have yet to undergo alien communication will benefit by learning from our common viewpoints about these encounters.

I am coming forward at this time to participate in the release of new information that is scheduled to help us have greater understanding of who we are, where we are going and what will soon come our way. Most people are no longer asking "if" things are happening, but rather "why" and "how." Along with this change, events that were once considered incredible are now being accepted as commonplace. There is a new receptivity to information about life outside our planet, beyond the third dimension of reality in which we live. It is my hope that this publication will be instrumental to those who want first-hand understanding of what it is like being in the presence of other forms of cosmic life.

Those of us stepping out now are somewhat like the early voyagers to the New World, providing letters that told of the land and people to those who stayed behind. Soon, I expect a multitude of undeniable incidents will flood our lives and books like this will no longer be needed.

It was a difficult ordeal bringing forth this information because I was concerned about the repercussions upon my life and professional credibility. I originally intended to write under a pseudonym to avoid attention and to protect my privacy. However, I was shown that anonymity is not part of the "bargain." I was told that revealing my professional background, academic credentials and grounded approach to life would enhance the credibility of the contents. As our cosmic friends prepare us to accept that they are here and have been for some time, they seem to find my ability to translate their communiqués about life, reality and universal laws appealing. I think they approve of the rational and logical approach I take with their information because it encourages consideration of what they have to say. My diverse experiences in medicine, science, and business have helped me to understand what I have been taught by other beings and in turn, enable me to explain their perspectives in ways that people can grasp.

By revealing this side of my life, perhaps people will realize that these things can and do happen to ordinary people. Nonetheless, I know there will be those who feel safer considering me unstable, lost in fanciful realms of fiction or unable to distinguish between true conditions of reality. This does not discourage me. I am prepared for whatever comes my way.

I admit, if I were not the author, I am not sure I would believe what appears in these pages. After all, tales about messages from unseen sources, visits from extraterrestrial beings and knowledge from spiritual entities seem like they should be science fiction fantasy rather than an account of what I have experienced. Yet despite my attempts to ignore and deny these situations, I know they have happened and are as real as any other activity in my life. I now realize it is not necessary to choose one reality over another; instead, the key is integration. It's time for all of us to recognize the truth that Kansas and Oz exist side by side; we need only change the focus of our momentary attention. We live in a multidimensional world that contains myriad possibilities. The only limitation is what we chose to recognize and accept.

The two parts of this book take different approaches to imparting information. Part One is a personal account of my struggle to reconcile and accept the events in my life, particularly the mysterious visits from many unknown beings. Part Two, the Teachings of the Spiritual Elders, contains information channeled from a consciousness much older and wiser than humanity. Their reflections about society offer guidance intended to help us grow. Interestingly, some of this information has been given in rhyming verse.

For those unfamiliar with channeling, it is communication from a source that joins the person speaking. Some people leave their body, like a trance medium, while others (like me) stay conscious and are aware of what is happening while in an altered state. Often, I am unsure of what is going to be said, but sometimes I sense it moments before the words are uttered. I can intervene at any time if I want to interject a comment but usually prefer to send my thought to the other entity and have it describe my viewpoint. When I channel, there is usually a feeling of powerful, unconditional love, coupled with wisdom and universal understanding. While in that state, I have access to fascinating knowledge about things I did not previously know about.

Besides the channeling, I have had significant face-to-face extraterrestrial contact throughout my life. Although I have repeatedly tried to ignore, repress and hide this, I must acknowledge the incredible gifts I gained through these experiences. These space travelers have taught me about many secrets of the universe that are based on scientific laws we have yet to become familiar with. At first I doubted whether the information was accurate, but after I began to search physics books and contemporary literature about alien encounters, I was shocked to find validation of what I experienced. I have seen their androids, time travel, processes to perpetuate mass illusions, genetic manipulation and even transfer of souls into clones. They have told me things about our government that I would not have believed if I had not heard later validating reports in the news. I do not have scientific proof of my encounters, and I probably never will unless they decide differently; I can only offer my personal account. However, I have often had knowledge beyond that of the general population, and those who know this secret side of me have sometimes sought me out for answers that might not readily be found elsewhere.

Now, I have been asked to come forward as one of many who will help our planet prepare for intergalactic communication as we enter a new phase of civilization. I have been told that a global effort is going to commence over the next few years to increase our awareness of other intelligent life forms. According to these others, they are preparing us for an unveiling of the truth about who we really are. This message was given to me in an abrupt and unexpected visit just days after the "Phoenix Lights" episode, when many people throughout the city reported sighting UFO's one evening. After a long reflection about the possible consequences of admitting to be a contactee, I decided to comply and participate. The details of what happened during this dramatic visit are described in the chapter *Contact Unveiled.*

How did I get to this point?

My dual life started at birth but was carefully hidden from others. When I was growing up, I told no one about my experiences. Who was there to tell? I endured visits from unknown beings that left me very confused, but there was no one to confide in. When I finally became a young adult and left home for college, I encountered a string of personalities who were involved in metaphysics. Many of these people harbored enormous and harmful egos, while others were downright charlatans. They were often uneducated and could not explain themselves in a rational manner; they presented themselves in ways that seemed to diminish their credibility. I ran away, not wanting to be associated with unstable fanatics.

These experiences resulted in a complete swing of the pendulum to the other side. I was dismayed by the irrational beliefs held by those I felt were unbalanced. As a result, I made sure I developed a strong foundation in common sense, intelligence and logic. I turned my back on my unexplained encounters and embraced conventional science and educational pursuits. I entered traditional medicine, beginning as a registered nurse, which led to a trail through healthcare administration. I earned a master's degree in business administration while running quality management departments for healthcare organizations; I also specialized in research, strategic planning and leadership training. Ultimately, I abandoned the corporate world to pursue developing a consulting business.

Ironically, I spent a large part of my professional life in "black and white" environments directing people to take all aspects of instinct and gut-level decision-making out of the work environment and instead taught them how to understand data and statistics. The formula approaches I taught from the total quality management movement helped many leaders improve their organizations. However, as my psychic abilities and spiritual awareness grew, it became increasingly evident that total reliance on hard facts was just as off-base as were knee-jerk reactions based on undeveloped gut feelings.

Along with this growing insight, I suddenly discovered guidance available from an unknown source that created much internal conflict. Channeling was, at first, unacceptable to me. As it later seemed to develop into a fad to which many people laid claim, I became even more reticent to get involved. Yet the information that came forth was very, very interesting.

Looking around at other published works brought confidence. Gary Zukav, Joan Borysenko, Judith Orloff, and Olga Kharitidi were members of science and the medical profession who wrote of other forms of consciousness and psychic situations. They were highly educated people, M.D.s and Ph.D.s who were literate and articulate. If the contents of their books were accepted, then mine was no more outrageous. And there were scores more stories shared by people just as well spoken and intelligent who worked in other established disciplines.

One day, a friend reminded me that having this knowledge from other worlds without sharing it with others was not necessarily honoring the intention of the communication. This insight brought me to a new perspective and this book was born.

Repercussions

As I come forward to speak about my paranormal experiences, I believe there will be three types of people who will react differently to what I present. These groups are not divided by race, nationality or religion, but rather by consciousness. I hope to help bridge the gap between these groups by explaining off-planetary experiences so others can be better prepared and integrate the information into their own belief systems.

The first group of which I speak are those who have experienced a strong spiritual awakening and will find the events in this book to be a matter of course, for they have their own experiences of equal merit and intensity, perhaps even more so.

The second group are those who are beginning to awaken. They have a mild-to-strong interest, often interspersed with a few out-of-the ordinary experiences, perhaps a near death experience, an encounter with someone who died, or strong instances of intuition or telepathy.

Finally, there are the hard core nonbelievers who cling to the tenets of a taught religion or pure intellectual pursuit. If it's not in the Bible or documented by NASA, then it falls somewhere between the devil's work and psychiatric delusion. I hope that they will choose to regard this manuscript as more than a bathroom accessory in the spirit of Voltaire, who once wrote to a man who offended him:

> *"Dear Sir,*
> *Currently I am seated in the smallest room in the house. I have your correspondence before me. Soon, it will be behind me."*

Like so many other stories, such as those written by Richard Bach or James Redfield, the chapters may be regarded as entertaining fiction or perhaps, just perhaps, another vision of truth. The choice, as always, is yours. I hope you enjoy the contents. I wish you blessings on your journey as you enter into mine.

Part One:

The Journey

Chapter One

Meeting The Others

Losing my fears

In my thirty-eighth year, I lost my fear of "things that go bump in the night." I don't know why, or what happened, only that I was no longer afraid. There were visits from otherworldly entities, rapping on the walls, and visions of events from different times since I was a small child.

Terror was replaced by serenity and peace. The odd thing is, I have no memory of why this change occurred, or what propelled a state of extreme alarm to change into calm acceptance. Perhaps being alone for a prolonged time allowed me to confront and dispel unresolved issues. When I finally learned about myself, the paranormal became normal, and I could embrace it rather than run from it.

Memories of other lives, knowledge about people and events not yet come to pass, voices without sound, seeing into other dimensions—I experienced it all and denied it, except to one or two intimate confidants. Many extraordinary events occurred, but perhaps the most pivotal concerned the messages that began to come through me.

It began innocently enough. While in a bookstore, a publication about channeling seemed to "pop" out from the shelf. I decided to give it a try. After buying a recorder and some dictation tapes, I practiced the exercises and gave it a whirl.

What happened next was amazing. The language was lofty, sometimes biblical. I would hear myself called "dear one, little one, my child," and other terms of endearment. I felt like a translator. As the messages poured through me, my brain quickly scrambled to find the right word to match the impulse.

On occasion, a chosen word would not convey the correct meaning. This was frustrating because I regard language as an art. I wanted to go back and edit the sentences, but felt they should be left in their integrity to avoid misrepresentation.

It was surprising to hear the tape reflect different characteristics of my voice. Cadence, inflection, tone, and depth would vary, which led me to believe that differing entities were the source.

The accuracy of the insights was uncannily correct. The information was often not about detailed aspects of my life, but generally focused on what was happening to the world on a spiritual level at the time. I stopped channeling when I was told that someone was going to make contact within two weeks but that did not come to pass. It caused me to question if I wanted to hear from that person, or if I made it up. Scared, I put down the recorder and did not channel again for a very long time.

Meeting higher dimensional light beings

When the channeling first began, I was curious about the source of information. "Tell me about you?" I asked:

> *We are beings of pure Light. We can manifest ourselves in different forms to show you the ways of the world. When you look at us and see us in a familiar manner*[1]*, it is more understandable to you and you can accept us better. Though with you, the Light is not unacceptable. You understand, you know, and are comfortable. And in some ways, you may be more comfortable with that than the shape of the one that you saw as Obadiah.* [2]

---

1 They are referring to when they assume human form.

2 Obadiah is the name of a male entity who showed himself during the first channeling.

Later, I requested a further description of the source and was told:

We are like a band, a troop of beings, but we are really one multidimensional aspect. It depends upon your interpretation and level of awareness. One being would see us as a group of brethren working together, where another higher being would see us as one higher level being with many aspects that can come together or go apart, as needed, to do the work.

No matter how fascinated I was by the information coming from within, there was always hesitancy about the messages. Thus it went slowly over the years. Between 1994 and 1995, I was given much encouragement by the channeling source to continue. Lectures that resembled a loving parent's encouragement found their way into the discourse:

You have the opportunity to transmit information that can be imparted to those who would benefit from it. We wish to work with you now to get (you) back to a point where you feel comfortable receiving the information and can step aside and remove your personal feelings, your personal fears, your blockages, and your difficulty with awareness of the things that affect you, so that you can be more effective for others who can benefit from the information. We would like to work with you to take away the fear that you have built up over recent time. There is much that we can impart that would be beneficial, much like a map helps the driver in the city, but we cannot go forth without your full permission and your willingness. You feel the rock, the barrier[3]*, and we cannot proceed without full willingness on your part.*

We will spend the next part of the future working to get back to a state of complete trust where you will allow us to come forth and give you the information, whether for yourself or for others, either by yourself or in the presence of others. You may then take what is imparted to you and sift through it and decide what you will give and what you won't give. Perhaps you like the job of the editor. If you choose, you may get yourself to a point where you will feel comfortable allowing us to speak to others through you. As this is one of your first preliminary attempts at it, you will be amazed at how fast things will

3 My resistance to communicating with them.

change for you. It is only to continue with the practice, and it is much like all other things of your world. They come so quickly, so naturally, and so smoothly once any skill or art is mastered.

You will be able to do great works for the people if you allow this to happen, but it must be your full and free choice. It is not something that we would push upon any being. It must be a willing and full partnership because it is based only in love. If there is discomfort or a need to push, it can allow other things entry which are less desirable. So you must stay positive and grounded in love and allow us to work with you, for it is our gift and is based in love.

The source provided information about world events and social changes, as well as guidance for proceeding through personal situations. Never specific directions, they were reminders about free will, aspects of reality, and other factors that can impinge on one's judgment when acting in response to events in life. After years of not understanding things that happened and who, or what, was present, a source was finally communicating with me in a way I could more easily comprehend. My trust increased as I was given valuable information to help me through difficult situations.

But how did I ever get to this point? So many other things preceded this breakthrough in contact with what I refer to as the Others and the Spiritual Elders. One of the most pivotal was the dissolution of the life I had safely hidden in to avoid memories of visitors not of this Earth. This was during my thirties, but if I am to be truly honest with this account, everything started at birth.

Chapter Two

In The Beginning...

Adjusting to my body

I was fully conscious as a baby and had to wait for physical development to catch up to my awareness. My gross and fine motor skills were restricted by the limitations of human neurological and musculoskeletal development, a frustrating experience for an awake, conscious soul residing in an infant's body. How difficult it was, anxiously awaiting to be able to speak the language of my parents rather than babbling gibberish. If only they could understand me. Would I ever mature? Such were the thoughts that circled my mind. And thus began my journey into the human experience.

My parents told me I was an unwanted child, a menopause baby who had surprised everyone. In fact, my father frequently referred to me as the little black pill that failed, referring to a morning-after abortion pill. There were two others before me, a boy and a girl. I guess I made the 0.8 in the quest to maintain the perfect demographic statistic of 2.8 children for the average household. The baby furniture and clothes had long since been given away. There were eight years difference between my sister and me, while my brother was six years older.

In those days, it was rare for this kind of situation to occur. My parents, although of average age by today's norms, were extremely old for child rearing. Everyone knew I was an "unexpected package" when they learned of the disparity in age between my siblings and me. Teachers would smile knowingly, revealing their thoughts ("Ahhh, another failed diaphragm"). Whoever would have thought that decades later women would fashionably give birth in their forties?

The immediate family knew I was a scared child, refusing to stay alone until they made me at twelve years of age. Most people attributed this to the stress of living in an unpleasant home environment with dysfunctional parents, never suspecting that the real cause was dread of alien visits. Perhaps there is wisdom in that all children are protected under the sacred guise of "imagination." No one believed me when I tried to tell them about the voices and beings in my room at night.

The earliest visits

I was confused each time I returned from my lessons with the Others. I would open my eyes, feel the sweat that soaked the small bed, then think, "this must home." But which life was real? Confused and scared, I cowered beneath the covers to wait for the safety of dawn and eventual sounds of my family waking up.

Each night they came. Before their visits, time was spent waiting, drifting between consciousness and slumber. Boredom was controlled by watching the flashing colored lights flying about the room. If one whorl rotated clockwise, I would make it go counterclockwise. Sometimes I would just send it flying off to another point in the room. Unbeknownst to me, these exercises with colored lights were homework left behind from my "guardians" to strengthen my psychic control. It took a lot of energy to redirect those luminescent shapes.

When this became tiresome, I quietly chanted numerical sequences. Favorites were two, four, eight, sixteen, thirty-two and sixty-four. In later years, I learned that the numbers I cherished as a child were recalled from another life when, as an initiate of ancient mystery teachings, I was taught about numerical mysticism. These digits were part of a formula to translate energy into matter; it was done by visualizing a universal pattern associated with each number, then chanting its associated sound.

Some of my visitors acted as teachers, while others observed me to study the human condition. Certain entities supervised my recall of different lives, while other ones guided me as I learned to travel through dimensions. There was a group of beings that were far more powerful than the others; these seemed to be highly evolved spiritual entities. They coordinated my teachings and arranged for me to learn about life in differing universes with diverse space races. The less dominant beings seemed to know that I was watched over by these others and because of it, treated me cautiously.

I noticed a definite hierarchy in the galactic world; it seems to be headed by very spiritual entities who lack physical bodies. They are pure energy and can manifest in any shape. They often assume a human appearance when making contact because we are most comfortable with entities who look like us. I call them higher multidimensional beings and there seem to be ranking orders within their stations. They have a consciousness that is simultaneously active in many realms of reality.

Despite my apprehensions, many of the events that happened were kindly and directed by one of these multidimensionals. A gentle, infinitely wise soul who would provide guidance many evenings, he seemed as if he was the embodiment of the universe. While I was wary of other entities, I had love and complete trust for this being. He portrayed himself as an old man with a long white beard and wore a tall hat, much like a sorcerer's. Peaked and midnight blue, it was studded with pictures of stars and crescent moons. This hat was for my benefit; while it delighted me, it served as a beacon to help me locate him in the realms of the universe when I needed assistance. I thought about the hat and suddenly I was with him.

We frequently went to a place in time and space where, in the vast darkness, there was a large region of light from no discernible source. I was often left alone, but could feel his presence off in the distance, watching as I went through my lessons. He taught me to travel in a multidimensional time-space continuum. The key is to retain conscious awareness and not think of oneself as a separate personality, disconnected from universal awareness. When I remembered I was an eternal being who was part of a concept known only as "all that is," I became part of an infinite cosmic consciousness teeming with knowledge. I instantly had any information I required. Spontaneously, I would appear wherever I needed to be, even if it was as a young five-year-old child waking up in my bedroom in 1963. The secret to dimensional travel is becoming one with God.

Most extraterrestrials are aware controlled thought is the passkey to universal globe-trotting and use this process as one of the ways to propel through space. With some species, their pilot's consciousness is tied to the alien ship's technology, like a living computer. When the navigator thinks of where to go, the ship manifests there as if it were a living body following a soul. Certain alien civilizations use sound frequencies to manipulate time-space for travel. They use tonal vibrations from trained entities who emit haunting singing tones. These acoustic energy patterns stimulate a ship's technology, like a key starts an ignition.

The usual routine

Many nights, I was taken away by a creature I called "Brown Bear." I would be on the precipice of sleep, and suddenly he would appear. I think he was assigned to help me understand different worlds, yet I never had complete confidence in him. I was always wary—was he teacher or captor? Could I trust what was being taught? I was suspicious of other life forms, never fully accepting that what they told me was the truth. This skepticism served me well in later years, when I realized that some species can, and will, manipulate us when they want something accomplished.

Alien life forms have the ability to obscure what really transpired and often leave behind recollection of animals rather than their unfamiliar faces. This is to protect us from our fears. It can be a shock, no matter how well prepared we may think we are, to be in the presence of extraterrestrials. Many people who have contact prefer not to recall being with an intelligent creature who lacks familiar humanoid features.

In this case, the image of a bear was a more comfortable remembrance than the strange appearance that was not humanlike. He was hairy, with brown fur and rounded facial features. In recent years I have seen a being who may be of the same species. He is a very hirsute, hybrid humanoid with shaggy long brown hair that is more like fur. He is also very kind and appears to be a teacher of some sort. If I heard him correctly, his name sounds something like Bereshid, if I translated it right.

Back in those days, I was often transported to a world where everything seemed backwards, a mirror image of Earth. (Or was it our world that was backwards?) It was always dark on that planet, with a different type of illumination than by our sun, yet it teemed with activity. It was just the opposite of a planet with life organized by sunlight.

Off in the distance, I saw mines surrounded by rocky cliffs, stripped land and smoke, perhaps from a smelter. Shadowy figures were led to quarry whatever bounty was being pursued. The workers were often hunched over wearing what may have been dark cloaks. They seemed sad and reminded me of bound slaves. I called them Black Bears because they resembled the Brown Bear, but they were much darker and somehow different in demeanor and function. I was afraid of them and never allowed to get too close.

Each night culminated in a presence before one I called "the King." He wore a golden crown atop his head but it was luminescent, like a halo of light. He was humanoid, tall and slender, possessing shoulder-length, golden-brown hair with a matching beard. He was different than the others and was near the top of the chain of command. He seemed like a spiritual being who was working with alien races. My lessons were usually with the Bear, but on rare occasions this taller presence would teach me directly.

I was often tested before I was allowed to return to my home on Earth. The King would quiz me about the lessons I had undergone with the Brown Bear or others. Often he and Bear would laugh at me and I would not understand why. Now I know they found me amusing when I asked simple questions.

Each time it was over, I suddenly found myself back in my bedroom. Somehow, I knew I had been released to continue my journey on Earth.

Until I was twelve years old, I would sleep under the covers, trying to hide from the visits. My parents would come in each night and uncover me to ensure I was breathing adequately. They attributed my bizarre ritual to childhood fears of nonexistent nighttime bogeymen.

Back then, I did not understand what was happening with my callers and as a result was fearful of the dark and being alone, which was when they usually appeared. I would quickly revert to behavior befitting a regular child after being with them and try to forget that anything happened to me. When I remembered, I regarded my visions as just bad dreams or my imagination, so I would not have to figure out which life was real. I recognize now that my fright helped to anchor their memories in my mind, so when I was ready to remember greater detail, I could retrieve important information.

This is a common method to embed knowledge in our minds. Information can be anchored in our consciousness by having something dramatic happen right after they teach us. They can put a person in a hypnotic state and instruct him about something for later release, back on Earth. After the lesson is over, they might gaze deeply into your eyes, burning the memory of their face into a place in deep consciousness. When you return to normal life, haunting memories slowly begin to appear of a strange creature with penetrating eyes boring straight into your mind. Alarmed and concerned, you return to those moments to decipher where they came from. At some pivotal time, more information is recalled, and eventually what was taught will be released.

Memories were planted for later release

The scenes I saw during those years were preparing me for when I would enter into the next phase of work with them, years later. It was planned that when I matured, I would be given knowledge that would contradict our history concerning the origins of Man. Not only was I (and the rest of the planet) being prepared to learn about alien contact with Earth, we were scheduled to discover proof that off-planetary beings were responsible for our creation and evolution. I was to be one of a contingency of people who would come forward to help deliver new revelations about our birth on this planet. Only I had to evolve to a point where I could accept that our recorded history was wrong and that man was not always the sovereign creature he is today.

It was going to take a lot of courage for me to abandon our teachings about human evolution, especially when the new information was unflattering, even heretical, to many factions. Years ago they burned people at the stake for inflammatory ideas; now if I spoke out contrary to popular belief, I would not face death but perhaps the contemporary equivalent: professional wrath, ostracism and ridicule.

Before readily abandoning my Earth's history, they would have to show me inconclusively over the ensuing years that the reality I knew was nothing more than an illusion. I would not accept, much less embrace, this information if it was given by intuitive insight or preaching lectures—and they knew it. Because of this, my life was filled with irrefutable proof that they existed and dramatic displays of events supposed to be impossible. Their plans to have me understand our role in the universe were laid out in a carefully timed sequence from birth to death. I had to completely acknowledge they were real before I would accept any information they had for me, especially if it would contradict my very life on Earth. They did whatever was necessary to get my attention.

I encountered visits from all types of beings, was taught lessons on places not of this Earth, experienced first-hand manifestation of objects, underwent one-way wormhole travel (then had to get back home) and much more. The early years were a struggle, trying to understand who I was and which life was real. Looking back, it was invaluable preparation to show me that man is not just a physical human, but is also a spiritual being who can unlock the limitations imposed by this life.

Those times were the first steps on a long journey. Next, I was scheduled to discover that we do not live just a single human life but are more complex beings than we seem.

Chapter Three

We Are Part Of A Larger Consciousness

When I entered adolescence, it was important to the Others that I understood each of us is just one part of a multidimensional consciousness that chooses to experience life in many ways. They wanted to help me understand that we undergo far more than a single human life. In addition to our Earthly experiences, we incarnate in physical, non-human bodies on other worlds and simultaneously exist in parallel dimensions and different universes. Beyond this, there are realms of consciousness that we are connected to but our human brains cannot fully fathom what the experience is like. All these other existences happen simultaneously but within their own place in space and time.

In later years, I was shown how to access these other aspects of ourselves. We can bring forth the image of a reincarnational self and have a conversation as if it were a guide. We can also merge knowledge by transferring our consciousness to theirs. When we connect, we can benefit from the personal work they have previously completed; if we grasp a lesson they already assimilated, we do not need to repeat it in our lifetimes. This way, we can save ourselves anguish by learning from their experiences.

Meeting my other selves

During my earliest teen years, they whisked me away to experience my other incarnations. Sometimes I watched as if I were viewing a movie, other times I relived certain incidents. By attaching my current life spirit to the former one I was simultaneously outside the body watching and inside experiencing everything first-hand.

Before I was introduced to my other reincarnational selves, I experienced an incident that seemed to make no sense until my first life remembrance was released. At age five, I screamed and ran away from an Egyptian sarcophagus at an art museum. When I walked by it, I was overcome with a foreboding presence that, if let in, would contradict what I had constructed as the safe reality where my consciousness hid during this lifetime. I cried hysterically and ran away. What seemed peculiar behavior at the time later became understandable when memories of my Egyptian lives were liberated.

When I was fourteen, I was escorted to a tomb in ancient Egypt where my recently dead husband had been laid to rest. The room was filled with items from our life together; there were many expensive looking objects encrusted with gold and gems. The vault was quite palatial. I was entombed with him—only I hadn't yet died.

I watched and relived my bewilderment. I could not understand how I could still be conscious and yet not move my body. Confused, I hovered around the sarcophagus that held my fresh corpse. After all, how could I be dead when I was still a thinking, reasoning being? Later, I learned that ancient Egyptian lore refers to this continuation of awareness beyond death as the Ka. It is an essence of our spirit that perpetuates beyond one's life.

Suddenly, startled and shaken, I was returned to my childhood room of this lifetime to wait for the safety and warmth of dawn. Years later, I was told by these teachers how to strengthen the Ka to perpetuate our existence after death. If we complete a series of breathing exercises done while visualizing patterns of colored light, we can leave our human body behind as we travel as a light form. If one is competent enough, after death, he or she can recreate the illusion of matter to replicate the body and seem physically real to others.

Countless remembrances released over those years. Ancient Egypt was a time of great learning and initiation and strongly tied to this life, as I soon learned.

In one incarnation, I was sitting on the edge of an internal pool, hidden in the bottom echelons of what appeared to be either a temple or a palace, as my teacher sat beside me. He was an old wise man, knowledgeable in many of the mysteries of life and the universe. As we talked, the Pharaoh's soldiers rushed in to kill us. The leader of that time wanted to remove all the temple priests who taught about secret knowledge that could unleash universal forces; he feared the power of these teachers. I was a rising and powerful initiate who was caught in the bloodbath. The blade of a soldier's sword was plunged into my abdomen, then twisted to eviscerate my internal organs, ensuring death. I clearly remember the stab. It began as a counter-clockwise arc from the bottom of the breastbone to the pelvis, continued straight up to the apex of the ribcage, then back down again.

During the viewing, the memory of the violence catapulted me back into my current body. I returned to consciousness as a confused and scared fourteen year-old child in my familiar 1972 bedroom.

These beings had me watch many lifetimes. One time I looked down and saw that my legs ended in the rough broad feet of an Egyptian peasant. He was lying on a dull gray hard floor where he slept. Bits of straw were strewn on the ground. It was the existence of an indentured servant, bravely enduring slavery. I discovered that I learned patience and humility from that existence, to balance an arrogance I had acquired in other times. There was the joy and pain of being a temple dancer who existed like a bird in a gilded cage. All my basic wants were attended to and my surroundings were quite lush. I discovered that my physical beauty during that life caused me to be a prisoner, forced to entertain others by dancing when instead I wanted to study and learn.

I saw when I was a dead prostrate body of an American soldier lying on my stomach, shot in the back. I was also once a dark-skinned African male walking along a jungle path, only to be startled and killed by a leopard and have my life end as part of the food chain. Prehistoric clan gatherings, Nordic travels, the Middle East, Greece, Rome, Germany, England, and France—these journeys and memories revealed themselves, story after story, for many years. Soon, I could see these lifetimes at will, without being escorted by visitors or entering into an altered state. Eventually, I discovered I had the ability to see the lives of other people, too.

I knew each continent and time, including civilizations of Earth for which we no longer have records or knowledge. These places held technology advanced far beyond anything we know. They were times when aliens walked openly among us and humans were of a different genus. We had a higher developed consciousness, allowing us to perform feats that would be considered miracles today.

One of my last life reviews was quite different. I was shown chaos on the Earth, coupled by catastrophic natural events: earthquakes; tornadoes; tidal waves, and much human suffering. I asked to be taken away with the others, through death or other means, for there was no enticement to live during those times. "No," they said. "You must stay and help rebuild, for we brought you here to help the children of Earth." This lifetime was not from the past. Eerily, I suspected it was tied to this incarnation. Only time will tell whether this fate is for our planet or a parallel reality. They have taught me well; I know it will be our consciousness that determines our destiny, not our technology.

That event haunted me as I grew older. It influenced my decisions for a while, until I tired of waiting. I convinced myself it was only a dream; I did not want it to be true and felt that denying it would lessen any potential for it to happen.

Meanwhile, my visitations continued. As I grew older I began to have more hints of what these other beings looked like. I heard voices and saw partial images while I was fully awake and was able to recall bits and pieces of encounters. I was always adamant with them that I would not remember what they looked like, yet it was getting closer to the time when I would be forced to abandon that demand.

Learning to fly

The visitors got more brazen as I aged. They arrived in the broad daylight of late afternoon rather than night or pre-dawn. Sometimes, I fought these encounters, often winning but not always. These episodes began when I felt a buzzing sensation in my head, followed by rigid immobility. It came on fast, within microseconds. It was as if my neurological command center had been circumvented, resulting in my body being incapacitated. I could not move until the controlling force left. While paralyzed, a voice, often female, would talk to me. I cannot recall what was said, but I think she tried to reassure me.

It was at this time that I was taught to astral travel. Oddly, it was done rather abruptly, like parents who threw me in the lake while shouting, "swim, swim!"

As I lay down to sleep one night, two robed beings with faces obscured by hoods suddenly appeared and unexpectedly pulled on my feet. I fell off the bed, confused. "What the heck was that?" I thought, as I tried to pick myself up off the floor. Suddenly, I became aware that I had ended up between the bed and the wall. "How could this be?" The bed was pushed tight against the wall, leaving just a fraction of space. It was impossible to fit in that small gap.

Without warning, I felt a whoosh and found myself hurtling through space, traveling through a place called the astral plane. This is a point of consciousness that is governed by different laws than the physical realm in which we live. It may seem chaotic, but it is just as real to those there as this life is to us here.

I saw beings seemingly unaware of me or their surroundings, as well as color and shapes looming around. There was a head hanging from a disconnected body; oddly, I had absolutely no fear, just wondrous amazement as I rapidly studied that place and my response to it. I noticed that I moved in accordance with my thoughts, rather than by messages sent to body parts. In fact, I was only thought, since my body was still in my bed.

I returned amazed. As I reflected about what I saw, I realized people who came back mentally splintered from hallucinogenic drug use encounter this space without being ready for it. It is where your thoughts control your reality and your fears become immediately manifested. A head dangling from a body can be horribly frightening, yet a person who has learned control will not have fear. Apparently, I was ready for what I saw, but others who force themselves into realms through chemical means may upset their psyche beyond repair and return dysfunctional. Prior to entering other realities, its important to have the tools and skill to control what you tap into.

After repeated times of being pulled from my body, I wanted proof that these incidents really did happen. I picked up a wrench lying in the grass as I passed through a yard when out of my body. I carried it around, determined I would bring it back to prove what had happened. I kept my attention on that tool the entire experience to ensure I still had it. As I began to translate back into my body, I felt my fingers spread apart. The gadget fell to the ground as I passed through the veils that part our worlds. I was frustrated that I did not have the personal power to transmute it back here. Years later, they showed me that things can be manifested into our physical reality, if one has the both the know-how and power.

Since I was often confused when out of body travel happened, I developed a test to help me recognize what was happening. When I was unsure where I was, I jumped up. If I floated down, I knew that I was not in my physical body but in the midst of some supernatural happening. It may sound silly, but we can get very disoriented during sudden paranormal experiences. Our attachment to our lives here can tell us something isn't possible even when it is occurring.

The mysterious hybrid bird

One situation was different. Suddenly there was the feeling that happens moments before the impact of a visit. I was paralyzed by forces beyond my control as a team of beings appeared while I lay motionless. They were veiled by the cloak of another dimension, yet the leader was a male figure who intentionally showed himself. His head was that of a bird, like that of a hawk, and he wore a headdress of some sort. I was measured with instruments not of this world that I can best describe as the language of color. When done, they left quickly, releasing the power that held me immobile.

I now realize that he resembled the Egyptian god Horus. I know from my work with many other life forms that his image could have been implanted to leave me a clue about who the visitor was. Or, this memory may be the exact representation of the being who was present.

Most of the life forms on Earth strongly resemble many extraterrestrial species that exist. Birds, reptiles, felines and others all have very advanced, intelligent counterparts. Our planet was once used as a playground for genetic tinkering by highly evolved non-human races. Many of Earth's species and phylum did not spontaneously generate or evolve here over time, but were genetic experiments left to see how they would develop in this terrain. The descendants that now roam this planet are the legacies of those experiments.

During those years, I experienced my other incarnational selves, astral traveling and bold visits in the midst of daylight. You see, no matter what happened, there was still a part of me that said, "impossible!" and was convinced that I had made it up. I became quite proficient at denial to hang on to what I wanted, which was a normal life. However, I had reached a point where I had to completely accept the validity of everything to continue learning about life in the cosmos. By the time I reached my thirties, I was being prepared for the next step. The other life forms were going to prove to me, beyond any doubt, that they were as real as I am. But to go forward, I would have to leave behind the life I had built.

Chapter Four

Proof Beyond A Doubt

They worked hard to prove that reality was no more than an illusory concept to help us live within a dreamlike setting. Almost every precept that we call normal was challenged. I faced entities talking through animal bodies; manifestation of objects across space, being taken to off-planetary places to deal with interstellar nuclear holocaust, and interventions upon my body for alleged repairs. Still, I denied that any of this was possible. It was just too outrageous.

Dissolution of my old life to prepare for the new

Before things became this extreme, I tried to hide from my life that society said could not be real. To protect myself, I created a socially acceptable existence during my later twenties and early thirties. I hid in a quiet marriage, living a classic suburban reality, right down to the utility vehicle and two dogs. Nothing was going to pry me out of there. At last I was safe—or so I thought.

Then one night as I lay in bed, I uttered to the universe, "I am ready for the next step." Someone somewhere heard me make that proclamation because my life changed within just months. Although I was ready for a transformation, I wasn't prepared that every aspect of my life would fall apart. I had no idea what I had done by making that fateful proclamation.

Soon after my declaration, I began a pilgrimage into the shadows of darkness. It was a series of events so odious, I had no difficulty walking away from the secure life I had built. I had spent almost ten years hiding from who I was and had steadfastly denied all memories of the visits. Encounters were rare and few over those years and I would not allow myself to even think about them. My psychic abilities dimmed as I ignored them and I steadfastly denounced anyone who expressed a belief in the supernatural. What better way to convince myself I was normal than to repudiate anyone else's claims of the abnormal? I became a self-righteous paranormal homophobe.

The alien visitors were not about to forfeit a valuable contact who had received such intensive training. It would be like losing a precious racehorse before it ever even got to the track. It was important that I open up and proceed to the next step of working with them. To do this, I had to let go of things that I tenaciously hung onto; things that seemed important but weren't, such as professional career growth and fitting into to a very ordinary existence. It would take embracing crisis to let go of my cozy existence and accept the new information and enhanced intuitive abilities coming my way. The Others knew this and something powerful was planned to draw me away from my cocoon.

Within months of silently telling the universe that I was ready for whatever was next, my life completely changed. The agency where I worked was dismantled and devoured during a reorganization. My job was eliminated. Unwittingly, I took a position with a company that had serious internal problems and I became the object of unwanted attention in a sexual harassment situation. Meanwhile, my marriage dissolved before my eyes. My husband and I had drifted apart; the time was right for us to end our union. The extraterrestrials had come back into my life, and I knew I needed to be alone to deal with these visits or find others who knew what it was like. I went through a divorce, work difficulties, financial stress, and the death of three pets. I felt alone, despondent, and overwhelmed.

Testing my boundaries

As events in my life deteriorated, profound supernatural incidents occurred, along with increased channeling. The Spiritual Elders, as I learned to call the ethereal teachers, came often to advise me and to provide guidance. They gave counsel about my increasingly hostile work environment, reminding me that it was all a drama to strengthen my resolve and character. They also were determined to show me whatever was needed to gain my confidence and prove they were as genuine as anything else in my life.

Using animals bodies

I awoke one night just before midnight to experience the impossible. An entity was speaking through one of my cats which was standing on the pillow. I was being warned of the situation with my boss. I was to be very careful because it would escalate into a lawsuit. Suddenly, the presence disappeared as the cat looked up mystified then jumped off the bed to reclaim her feline body.

This left me dazed. Animals don't talk. They may give poignant looks, even telepathically send a message, but their brain-larynx connection does not accommodate human speech. I was profoundly disturbed. It was difficult enough hearing other entities communicate to me inside my head or in my room at night when they visited. Now Socrates my female cat not only spoke but was prophesizing. I am unsure how the Others did this; I suspect they either projected their voice so it seemed to be coming from her or they actually entered her consciousness and used her voice box.

Manifestation

Incidents continued as the Elders tried to provide me with constant proof to accept the validity of their presence. Arriving home one evening, I discovered I had left my computer disk containing the diary of my boss's offending actions and dates at the office. To compound the issue, the next day I was supposed to be in an early morning meeting in another city one-hundred-twenty miles away.

I took a brief walk to calm down. In the midst of the trek, I decided to drive back to the office that night to retrieve the computer file. Suddenly, there was a strong warning not to go; there was an element of danger. I questioned what type of danger and saw a vision of a car accident on the freeway, followed by a scene of me on a ventilator at one of the local hospitals. I argued with the Others, refusing to stay home, denying this could really happen.

"If you are who I think you are, then you have the power of manifestation. You can bring that disk here to avoid my going downtown to the office. Otherwise, I will take my chances and go," I challenged them.

I walked in the house and looked in my briefcase again. The disk was there in plain sight. Stillness gripped my heart. Never before had anything of this magnitude happened. Despite the petition, there was never any expectation of it being fulfilled.

I went into the backyard, where I heard the Others lecture on the danger of not heeding warnings:

> *There was extreme doubt and you were not listening to the messages you were receiving. We could not take the chance on an adverse event, so to speak, happening to you. What you requested was then granted, for you would not listen, and you need to learn to HEED what is said to you. Yes, that was somewhat of an amazing event tonight, but it was necessary. Do not test us too much, for we do not wish to waste our time on such trivial matters. And again, heed what is said to you and you will go far and fast.*

Noise, pranksters and missing time

My home was getting noisier as they the walls snapped, crackled and popped with communication from beings trying to get my attention. The solitude of sleep was broken one night by the sound of a rapid, intense, repetitive drum beat in my room. Another time I was jolted from slumber by a crack as loud as a thunderclap emanating from a dresser near the bed.

I once heard a lecture on other-worldly entities, cautioning we had only to pay attention to the soft caresses and touches of energy they shared. "I should be so lucky," I thought. I was being pulled at and grabbed while in bed. There were times when my limbs would go flying in a manner similar to the spasms seen with multiple sclerosis and other neuromuscular afflictions. I had no doubt this was not disease related. There were never any feelings of fright, rather more of playfulness, like a reminder we are here. I say we, because my intuition told me it was not just one being.

There was another strange incident with one of my cats. She was sprawled out on one end of a coffee table, eyeing a rose on the other side when there was a sudden peculiar "blip" in my consciousness. The next thing I knew, she was facing the other direction and had a different expression on her face. It was like a rough marker was clumsily left behind for me to recognize something odd had just happened. Something was different, but the only evidence that anything might have happened was a few things positioned askance. My slight confusion was a teasing hint that someone had made a visit.

Years before, something similar happened. I stood talking to staff members in a small office. I was standing in front of a round table while others were sitting. Suddenly, I felt my head violently crash down upon the desk. The next thing I knew, I was still standing there talking to them. Apparently, nothing happened. Yet I know I felt my head hit the desk as I got bumped from behind then yanked back up to a standing position. I chalked it up to a vivid imagination while silently questioning my sanity.

Technology beyond our time

During contact with the other beings, they have shown me technology that has not yet been invented here. One small machine similar to a laptop has tremendous potential to change our lives. An object that looks like a compact disk is placed inside a slot to start some type of a program where a hologram appears.

Somehow, incidents (such as epochs in time) are translated into sound, like some type of sequencing pattern, then compressed into a memory that is held on these disks. When a correctly coded frequency that sounds like a harmonic tone is played, it initiates the hologram. Oddly, it is the human voice using tonal qualities, that activates this device.

A person must be trained to reach a particular tonal frequency to trigger the process. To protect the device from unscrupulous access, this sound is attained by reaching a powerful emotion of purity and loving innocence. When the correct combination of oscillating frequencies is achieved, a scene is generated that is entered for travel to different dimensions and time periods. By stepping inside the picture you can learn from the events it contains. Perhaps we only have to wait for the right person or team with the technological capability, resources and funding to bring this particular apparatus into our current lives.

Dimensional travel and lessons in cosmic holocaust

One visit was extraordinary. Taken aboard what appeared to be a ship, I met beings who were high-level teachers. They notified me that a nuclear holocaust had just occurred in another dimension. I did not understand why I was there—what did they want with me?

Suddenly, it became apparent what they desired: my task was to stop the wave impulse and prevent energy from going to other dimensions, including Earth's orbit. I learned it was my responsibility to contain the situation. I had to prevent the shock force from disrupting life forms in other galaxies and time frames.

I was trying desperately to avoid disaster by programming a machine like one of the holographic units described above. I had to emit a particular intonation in synchronization with the device. The entities kept reminding me of the power of sound's vibrational frequency while they directed me to use the tonal qualities of my voice.

Unfortunately, my voice kept faltering, and I could not achieve the correct tone. I was frustrated and could not understand why this skill wasn't working. They tried to help by telling me something that to this day I do not understand, "I want you to remember the "ballet-aterium." At least that's what the word sounded like phonetically. It was a hint to help attain a point of vibrational frequency. Unfortunately, it didn't work and only left me perplexed.

I was anxious beyond imagination. After trying hard to get the machine to work without success, the teachers appeared and said, "It's only a play, and this dimension will disappear. You cannot save it."

Their answer was a possibility not previously considered in my dire efforts to save all those lives. An entire dimension of beings was eradicated —this was unfathomable and unacceptable to my human belief system. Suddenly, after I was given that information, they returned me to my bedroom at 1:15 a.m. to record my memory of the incident.

But it was not over. They soon came back and took me away again, this time to test what would be remembered. It was imperative the incident be readily retained and retrieved and not lost in memory. There was much confusion; these realities clashed with consciousness as I knew it, leaving me feeling disjointed.

An indecipherable background noise played in the background as "loora, loora" was softly and melodically chanted over and over. I was once again abruptly returned to my body, consciousness and bed at 8:30 a.m., where I quickly recorded on tape everything I could remember about what just happened.

Later, I read of an alleged planet called Lyra in the Pleiadian star system that, according to the author, was destroyed long ago. I cannot help but wonder if it was not "loora, loora" that was being chanted, but "Lyra, Lyra," to leave me a clue about something that happened in another time. Perhaps this incident was a warning to steer us away from nuclear cataclysm.

Surgical repairs

I continued to have guests. Roused from sleep in the early dawn hours, I heard two male voices talking. They struck me as doctors from a different dimension whose conversation was uncannily similar to a consultation between a general practitioner and a specialist. I overheard them speaking about my left eye having "hydratic cleaves." At least that is what it sounded like.

The next thing that happened was a black and white disk was rotated and spun to a high frequency until a laser beam was emitted. As odd as it seems, a procedure was completed to repair whatever ailed my left eye. But what was wrong with my eye and how could this intervention from another dimension repair it? How can a black and white disk be spun to emit a laser beam? Who was responsible for this? I never found out what was wrong and did not detect any apparent difference afterwards.

Different brain centers

During one encounter, a life form introduced itself to me and took action to show how we differed. Telepathically, the being conveyed it wanted me to see something, then came near and I was able to look inside its head. While we have an organic tissue-based mass for brain matter, the correlating organ for this entity's brain was comprised of crystalline cylinders. Suddenly, these differently pigmented sections began to emit rays of colorful light that circled each sector. When I asked what it was, they said it was the pattern they expressed when love was emitted. Could this life form have been a hybrid that was part biologic and part computer? Somehow I suspect it was.

Insanity or a new understanding of reality?

Their phenomenal displays were persistent; every day or night something amazing transpired. I know that some people may regard these occurrences as no more than fanciful illusions or perhaps even symptoms of mental illness. Yet I am grounded, well balanced and readily integrate into society as a productive member. As we learn more about ourselves and open to up to new realities, incidents such as these will not evoke fear and amazement, but rather an intense curiosity to learn more about these situations. When I was experiencing trepidation for revealing the contents within these pages, the Elders added the following message to this chapter.

> *Each reader will find their own barometer of truth in the words set forth on these pages. It is not for you to worry as to the contents, for our purpose is to shake the nature of reality by providing a dichotomy of presence: you, with the radiance of rational intelligence to awaken a curiosity factor in the doubters. Will there be repercussions? Perhaps, but remember that all events in life are programmed for the growth of the individual and nothing will come your way that is not a "special delivery," so to speak, designed to help you in your understanding of the journey of life through the human evolution.*

Personal despair opened up new doorways

The despair that I went through with my difficult personal situations helped me to stop resisting experiences with these other beings. I was so depressed that I had very little energy left to fight them. Besides, the Others were pretty much all that I had since I despondently withdrew from everyone around me.

In retrospect, I learned priceless lessons. Those years were a time when my character and strength were tested; the situations that brought me heartache also helped me grow. Rather than fight the things that happened to me, I learned to accept these predicaments and saw them as an opportunity to test my spiritual maturity. Most importantly, the hostile work incident gave me the strength of confidently withstanding personal attack.

I learned to respond to foolishness in a dignified manner and discovered that if I remain balanced, I can thwart the power of an angry person's aggression. These painful situations taught me ways to deal with angry people in public settings.

I had no idea how important this was going to be and that this was just preliminary training for what was to come. Little did I know there were plans for me that were yet to be revealed, that in the future, I would come forward to speak about my contact experiences in public. They were guiding me through circumstances to prepare me to stand in my truth in unpopular situations.

All these occurrences left me uneasy and curious, yet I was no longer scared. I began to feel very comfortable with these mystical events, perhaps more so than the world that seemed so hostile.

Chapter Five

Messages Of Encouragement

I continued to allow messages to come in as time passed by, and I struggled with the events in my personal life. It was 1994 and looking back, there is now greater significance to their words than when they initially began communication.

The messages were always encouraging; a mixture of benevolent love coupled with gentle hints of events to come. These discourses repeatedly emphasized that I was to overcome the fear that was constantly invading my life. So many of their explanations centered on parallel realities and the infinite possibilities created by free will. I was taught about the illusion of time and space, but I did not fully realize it at the time.

What amazed me were the classical biblical references. "The Father, the Lord," were terms I would never use. I might refer to a Creative Source but would never use traditional religious terminology because it seemed so condescending. Yet these terms kept resurfacing, and I was constantly referred to by childlike endearances, the kind one would picture an old great aunt using. To hear the term "little one" come from my vocal chords in reference to myself was, well, amusing at best.

My personal beliefs are that events in life are not by random chance, but are brought into being for further growth in our journey to be a more loving human being. External circumstances come about in a cosmic quest that provides opportunities for growth.

Adversity leads to strength

In the midst of it, I did not understand why my difficult work situation continued. What was I not seeing that continued to lock me into such a ridiculous drama? Why did I continue to participate in it?

"Explain these events," I asked. "Help me to have greater understanding."

As we have said, we want you to have greater understanding, to learn and to grow. The twist of events, or new course of events from which you can learn, keeps you sharp and helps get you ready for new events that will soon be brought your way with major life and Earth changes. It is but an exercise, much like the physical exercise that you know and experience to keep you in shape, to keep you sharp and to help make you as fit and prepared and ready as you can be. We are but your trainers in the current time and our purpose is to make you strong so that you can be a servant of the Lord, and to provide the greatest light through your strength, knowledge, and wisdom, which you are now honing in your preparation for future work.

Time to pause for reflection. Intellectually, I could understand that the more situations l learned to handle, the greater benefit I could be to others under stress. Having undergone adversity, my heart would be more open to compassion. Where I previously tended to disbelieve unordinary situations that didn't meet the expectations of June Cleaver, the fictional perfect sit-com mother from a 1960's TV show, time had taught me that bad things could happen to good people.

Another time, they warned about work getting worse.

Your course of events shall change while you go into intense training at this time. The lessons will be deep and hard. We will help you to balance the needs of the work environment with day-to-day life. You have faced such challenges before and will continue to do so. So have faith, that is the most important thing. You have always pulled though and, there is no reason to doubt that you shall be able to do so at this time.

Channeled entities have different purposes

I continued to wonder about the changing voice. It reminded me of when in the seventies, I had heard an older woman speak who professed to be a medium. The characteristics of her voice changed as an entity she called Stephen spoke through her. There seemed to be some similarities between their voices and I asked about this.

The memory is from the sound of the voice as it translates through you, for the cadence is similar and the delivery is similar. Stephen was one who traveled the planes but we are not of this one, although there are memories and similarities. For we come from a different area and have different knowledge, purpose, and capabilities.

Their companionship over human contact

During that time I had isolated myself from the world. I asked about my loneliness.

There will never be loneliness, for we will be with you always. We always have been with you and you are only just beginning to recognize that now. You are beginning to bring us forth through the voice, and it is difficult for you. We are always there and we speak to you in your mind. We are like a collective unconscious. As you have just begun to realize, there is more than one of us that is working with you. This is new to you in many ways but in many ways it is not. For as we have just told you, we have been there since you have come down to Earth. Different ones have come to work with you. They have stepped in and they have left, and this will continue, dependent upon your needs and your learning at the time.

Do not forsake us and do not be lonely. For we may not be of human spirit and form, but we can give you much that the humans cannot. And that is what you have been seeking all along, and we know that you realize that.

We will present and bring forth to you experiences that will bring the richest knowledge and help you to make the best decisions. We have always guided you and will continue to do so, though you may make decisions that will not always be in your highest interest. We will do our best to guide you, but you, like all others there, have the free choice to choose your alternate path. So choose wisely, my little friend, choose wisely.

Propelling others to seek

At a later time they suggested I was going to work with others to help with their personal learning quests and spiritual journeys:

> *We are here to work with you. Although there are others who fall under our domain, you are the one who is of focus now. You are going to go retrieve the others by serving as a catalyst for their awakening. And that has to do with your doubt, for in your doubt you are going to seek, and you are going to question, and you are going to share. We will guide you through this so that there will be no great mistakes or harm done to others. The questioning, the sharing of information is going to spark others to question themselves and to query whether to begin their journeys on the path. Not the path of life for which they are here and will partake but the path of higher learning for which they may now petition.*

Earth changes

One evening in 1994, I was surprised when they started with a question: Did I want to direct the discourse by posing questions, or just allow the information to come through?

> *Hello, my friend, we are here. Before you partake on your journey for this evening have you any questions? Would you like to set the stage or go free?*

I suggested that they just pursue their agenda. They began to speak about the potential for Earth changes, as well as my direction in life.

> *We are well pleased in your progress. You have made great strides in a very short time. We knew that you would, for we have always had faith in you. There will be interesting things coming your way and the lessons and the tests will continue. Have faith and do not falter, for you have done so well, and you will continue to do so. Abide by the love that you know and you feel, you hear and you see. It will guide you accordingly. Do not lose faith, for great things are coming and we will be there for you. To tell you any more at this time would alter events.*
>
> *You are doing well and you will be able to have more knowledge. But we must make sure that you can continue the strength. And for this we will watch and will see. We love you and know that you love us. And those bonds will keep us going forth to do the work of the Father.*

As far as the changes, no it is not settled. Of course it is not settled.[4] *But the tilt is there and the course of events now make it a probability that the changes will occur. We will see. There is great likelihood that the food shortages that have been predicted will come about. Job markets will change but most people now have the ability to see what is happening in the world of business.*[5] *Your gift of healing will come about; you are confused for you thought you were to travel the path of business. And now the healing is coming back again. And you have also felt us within you. Something that you felt you would not do, would not share.*[6] *But it is done with love and it is done gently to get you accustomed to the ways of us so that you can work with us stronger and more closely.*

Do not have fear. The experiences will become more familiar and will become second hand. If you continue to progress at the rate and the speed with which you have, this will all be done quickly and we will be on our way.

The practice of recording and writing is beneficial to you, do not stop. In fact, continue to practice and partake of this more. It will become much easier for you the more that you do. Have directed dreams this evening, for we will have you take back the messages that you need to keep. Good night.

Atmospheric interference

There were a couple of times when it was difficult to conduct the session and I did not understand why. They addressed this by referring to poor atmospheric conditions. I later learned that weather patterns and radio, TV and satellite transmissions can interfere with their messages.

It is difficult to make contact tonight; the conditions aren't optimal. Therefore, we are having difficulty with the transmission and you can

---

4 This refers to my silently voiced thought about whether the Earth changes that so many others had predicted for the turning of the millennium would occur.

5 The time was 1994, and they were referencing the massive layoffs as companies responded to external forces and profit losses.

6 This concerns the cohabitation when working with them. I had always thought that if mediums were legitimate and did allow other entities to take over their body, they must be insane to do so.

feel this because the strength is so much weaker, which also affects the receptivity of the channel[7] *who listens to us.*[8]

Releasing fear opens doors

In 1994, they spoke of possible changes for events already tentatively established. Information came through in a series of sessions, such as:

My dear, do not have fear of us, for we come to you only in love and to help you to gain wisdom in your travels on the Earth. There are many things of which we could speak at this time. You frequently wish to know of the situations that pertain to your personal life and the unfolding of the dramas that surround you on that level. Yet you question what's happening on global levels. Why are we here working with you, and what is about to happen? And yet unless you release that fear and allow us to speak forth, the blockage will be there and the information will not come to you. So you must make a conscious decision of how far you wish to go at this time and how much you wish to know for us to be able to impart information to you. That is something you might wish to think about. For we are ready, whenever you are ready.

Earth changes

How interesting it was to hear myself quoted of phrases I had previously used when speaking to friends. It had a jarring effect, as if to say, "we are with you always." We hear, see and know everything.

The changes you want to talk about are applicable to all. Your coining of the phrase "Pre-Millennium Syndrome" (PMS) is rather apt. It is not as much the changing of the years, it is the conditions that are correlated with the passage of time. For the electromagnetic configurations upon the Earth are changing due to planetary configurations. This of course in turn, affects all other places upon the Earth: the oceans, the land, the winds, and the forces of nature that

---

7 They are referring to me.

8 Since the signal was feeble, my ability to pick it up and translate it was impaired.

must mix together to create the planetary weather and conditions that you experience.

You must use your awareness to the highest degree. For you will be able to navigate, while others will just be able to react, to respond, to use a phrase. We will continue to give you information but the greatest information you had was back in April, your time, when you heard the voices before you knew what was happening to you, and you heard the telling of what was occurring.[9] *You have heard this morning people speak of their lives in turmoil and change—this is a mass effect. You will be instrumental in helping others because you have understanding of yourself.*

They continued:

We have spoken before to you of great changes that are coming and are being manifested at this time. And it is being felt oh so strongly. Especially among those with the ability to receive stronger than others. And you can sense what wave is coming in, in the future. There are general tides of great change, and technology is making its impact as it rolls through the time that you live in. Others are aware the way of life will be changed in the near future and upgraded to a style of communication that the masses have not been used to.

In many civilizations there have been many mechanisms of communication. This is one where your people shall use interactive methods such as the computer, the television, the telephone and the marriage between such. With these changes shall come a revolutionary alteration in lifestyle. There will be those who have, and those who have not. A great chasm, a great gulf will occur between those who can travel in the new mode and those who cannot, or are unable. As we have mentioned before, it is an acceleration for humanity that is occurring at this time. You and those around you feel the pressure of the changes as they come through more strongly and manifest. How you choose to take that energy and interpret it and use it in your personal dramas differs a bit for each.

---

9 This was one of the first events and I did not know what was happening. A voice was speaking in my head, telling me about impending Earth changes. Frightened, I lost all of the information because I did not think to track it. I was more concerned that I might be losing my mind.

This includes you, but you have put yourself in a most difficult spot, for you barely can climb up out of the mud pit that you have fallen into. You are tired, you are not using your wisdom and your strength and your power.[10] *You know better than what you have been doing. You, of all people, have the tools and the knowledge and should be one who is guiding the others. Instead you have fallen right in beside them. So you, too, must make your own choices: whether to stand up and be a leader or to swim beside the pack and be no different and accept the repercussions of whatever comes your way.*

Everything has a purpose

They continued to lecture me during another transmission and included an explanation as to why my life seemed so difficult and out of control with divorce, work harassment, isolation, and painful emotions.

Let us speak of the issues, for it is of those that you have also asked to have discourse tonight. The tests as we have said get harder and more furious, and they are more difficult to undergo. You are in the midst of a significant wave of events which is impacting the progress of your life. They are coming at you rapidly and with great intensity. You have decided to undertake many things and overcome them quickly to get onto other pathways in your life.

That is why there are so many multiple dramas with great difficulty. For the lessons must be learned and must be accomplished before you can pass on to the new areas. That is why you are enduring so much, and it is so difficult, and it is wearing you out. You know and we know that you have the strength to overcome these and as quickly as you would like. It is no one but yourself that holds you back for in many ways you are your own greatest enemy. You know you have the capacity to go anywhere you wish to go and to accomplish anything you wish to accomplish to bring forth the events to you which you need. You have the higher knowledge to direct events to those as you wish, so long as your motive remains pure. But once you stray from that, then other events will be brought to you to bring you back into focus.

---

10 This was in reference to my difficult work situation.

Hidden messages and lessons about time

One very hot summer day, I went for a walk. For some unexplained reason, I looked below just as my foot was about to come down on a young rattlesnake. I froze, backed away and ran toward the street.

A man came along and saw my distress. He went over to where the snake was. It remained there, lying complacently. He began to throw pebbles at it and I felt great remorse. The snake wasn't hurting anyone; there was no need to antagonize it. It coiled, rose up and hissed, then finally slithered away.

That night, I decided to ask why this encounter had come my way. A portion of the message contained a warning for me pertaining to the unpleasant work situation described previously. The session ended with information about the influence of present events upon past and future times. It was my first introduction to the tenuous nature of reality and how linear time is continuously impacted and changed.

As all things on this Earth are symbols and messages for those who have the ability to see them, this was an illusion chosen to convey a particular thought. The snake is associated as a sign of wisdom and higher learning and is often regarded quite highly in mystical circles. We knew that this image would be recognized by you. Coming so close without recognition was a warning to watch closely all around you. Events will unfold on different levels, and you must take the information and integrate it into meaning for you. You came so close to a situation that could potentially have danger. But you knew not how the snake would react.

And did it not just lay there and have no response to you? You felt remorse at the one who threw pebbles at it and it would have been best to speak up to support the peace of the being who lent its energy to convey the message to you. But that little one shall go on and is now on its way to its other journeys. So the message was to watch all around you, pay attention, particularly to the learnings on ALL LEVELS. Like the parables of the one who walked the Earth a long time ago[11] *information is imparted at the level of those who receive it and the*

11 Jesus

same information can be interpreted in many, many different ways by different people.

Again, integrate, watch, and carefully build your own set of reality that has meaning to you. These instances that still amaze and shock you will continue, to get the message across to you. For this is how you have communicated that you need to see information to accept it. It still must come as a bit of a shock to you to get through to all levels for you still deny so very, very much.

In this way you try to return to the life that was safe and known to you but you have set forth and there is no going back. There is "not going forward" but there is NOT going back. For what was once, is no more. As we travel the path of knowledge, learning and what you perceive as time, instances continue to change. And it is true when one recognizes that one cannot go home again. That is because the dramas and situations have changed due to the influence of present, current and even future events upon those paths so things will never be the same. There may be different paths to choose to take and to walk upon, and some may be more parallel than others and emulate the former image that you once knew. But it is not the same image.[12]

Time isn't linear

In a later message they added more information about "time." They continued with information about multi-tracking consciousness and closed with a scolding lecture:

Events will begin to pop forth now, ones that have been planned long ago; it is their time. They shall erupt to the surface in a manner that will allow them to manifest and bring about the actions that need to occur. This will be a pivotal time, an important time. Though each day will seem slow in its passing, there will be something there that will have bearing on what you know as the future; we know it all as

---

12 Contrary to our beliefs, the past is not static but always changing based on our decisions and the actions we take in our current lives. You can never return to the past because it no longer exists as you knew it. We are constantly creating different parallel existences, and some of them are quite similar to our current lives. By "not going forward" they mean that we may trick ourselves into believing we can avoid the future by taking no action in our lives; however, even no action has a result and will ultimately propel us into a future reality.

one. No past, no present, no linear time. All simultaneous, all multiple pathways with probable and different results that occur at once, that shape and evolve beings to the highest level possible.

The focus of attention in the human form is on one particular area of concentration; those are the images that you draw forth and (from which you) build your current set of reality.[13] *As the mind is designed, it can process only so many things at one time, except in the cases of higher evolved beings who can multi-track their minds to take in multiple levels and sensory perceptions. You can do that in the beginning stages, as you have learned throughout the course of your life. You are at the evolutionary path now where you can multi-track. We are using one of your words, and we know that you recognize it as such. You have not yet learned proficiency or excellence in this area, but you have the capability and have demonstrated as such. In time, the experiences will improve and the products will be better. Like all things, practice makes perfect.*

Events in the world shall continue to erupt, but there shall not be a major action of significance that will tilt the course of events at this time. You shall still be going forth and learning the lessons of a personal nature at this time-that is what the rest of this year is all about. The players shall come forth and fill their parts and help to build toward the future. Enjoy the beauty that is brought to you and do not dwell on what you perceive as disappointment; it all serves its purpose of higher growth and learning.

It is not the drama and events, but it is how you proceed and process through with your lessons. We know that you know that, for you have tried to teach that lesson to others as well. But do not forget that it also applies to you, and though you contend with the difficulty of human emotions, work them through to the highest level possible for you and you will proceed.

---

13 Refers to how each person draws to his or her self certain circumstances to develop the personal growth that is important at the time.

Timelines

They spoke of timelines and higher realms:

Timelines that we have are much like the timelines that you use for projects. They are updated, they're changed, they're shortened, they're varied, they're flexible but they are there. Don't forget to use them as an efficient and effective tool for guidance, but they are only timelines and nothing else.

Unconditional love

The Source also had words during a discussion about unconditional love:

The grandiose lesson of unconditional love, the highest, most elevated lesson known to man. For with unconditional love, one can walk all planes and go all places. For you bypass the lower emotions of the levels of man. This is a great lesson.

Compromised motives

They then gave a lecture about manipulating events:

You are going forth to quickly conquer this[14] *to be able to have a path that you hope will be your reward for achieving this lesson. But that is not the reason to do this, for in unconditional love you must just give forth and not try to manipulate the future. But remember what we have just said to you: if it is your purpose to create an outcome, then that is not unconditional love.*

Learning to harness energy

On Thanksgiving Day, 1994, Source gave the first intimation about the potential to harness available human energy and redirect it for a higher purpose. They showed me that I could use certain exercises to collect energy and send it to a nation in distress.

The messages shall come through as they are needed, but you should still practice to become proficient at taking back the information in a manner that makes sense to you and to others who may learn

14 A situation I was trying to manipulate.

from the teaching. This is a great day upon your Earth in the area of your country for it is a day when most of the people gather together in a harmonious environment to give thanks. Therefore, there is much positive energy that can be harnessed and used to the benefit of mankind and other species who dwell upon your planet. You may wish to focus in and to help direct that positive type of energy in a manner to be used most constructively for a higher purpose, for a higher good. Choose whether you would like to direct the energies but concentrate beforehand for you will receive divine guidance in this area to help you focus it in a place where there is need.

All illnesses have specific messages

I believe ailments are not random, but serve as "wake-up calls" for issues that plague us. A pain in my back had lingered for some time; I asked why I had brought this on. The Elders' words addressed my reticence to let energy flow unimpeded regarding what was happening.

In regard to the pain in the back, think carefully about the location and the reason for hanging on to this discomfort. It is affiliated with the base of the spine through which energy must flow. An incorrect alignment is equal to a disruption in the flow of the energy that goes through the spine and up into the rest of your body.[15] *Until you work on the other areas that are disrupted, you will not feel a peacefulness within the musculoskeletal system of your frame. So now you have understanding of where the true problem lays. And it is for you to go to work on the issue.*

Acceptance into the academy

In a vivid dream in September of 1994, I was in a bookstore and given an old, rare book which was color coded five ways. The colored sections were drab, muted hues of saffron yellow, olive green, blue gray, dull orange, and pale red. A sacred document thousands of years old, the colors

15 They were telling me that I was impeding energy that should have been allowed to travel freely through my spinal column. My resistance to their teachings and energy transmissions was manifesting as physical back pain to make me aware of what I was doing to myself. Once I let my resistance go, the pain would disappear.

corresponded to certain types of lessons within those pages. One color was interspersed with the other sections, signifying that those lessons were woven throughout the others. I cannot recall, but intuition cautions that those lessons centered around love. The pages were not paper or parchment but a substance not of this world. I balked that I did not want the book because the content had already been gone through once. "But this is the new and improved version," the Elders cajoled. I finally relented.

Right after, I was taken to an Eastern Indian Master, who had long, dark, wild hair and brown skin. His eyes were indescribable, a cross between insanity and enlightenment. They were so brilliant with light I could not see any pupils. Oddly, there was a smell of incense in the air. Other students were present, but they could not be seen clearly.

A name shot through my consciousness. I heard them say "Lord Maitreya." I sincerely doubted there was a connection between the name and the being described above. The Source told me:

> *The one that you think, that you suspect is with you, is. You have been accepted as a pupil but you can be bounced out, so to speak, at any time, should you not meet the requirements, the discipline of the position.*
>
> *You have a name and you are rejecting the name because you feel this cannot be true. You do not accept as valid yet the entire circumstance. We will wait until you are ready. You have the information and more will be brought to you.*
>
> *Do your best, for we are proud of you and hope that you continue to excel. We would not have brought you to this one if we did not feel that you were not worthy of the cause.*

I seldom saw these spiritual teachers except for a rare hazy vision. When they appeared as humanoid, their features were odd, with broad faces with modestly slanted almond eyes. They were often bald and resembled an old Tibetan monk in a white robe. Sometimes a gold sash was present. Oddly, although they seldom used names, when they did they took biblical ones, such as Obadiah. During these years, I began to meet many other life forms who slipped through the dimensional folds to visit our planet. I had no idea the universe was comprised of such a wide range of beings who had advanced civilizations. I was about to learn much more about some of them.

Chapter Six

Who's Out There?

The cosmos is teeming with life, far beyond your wildest imagination. There are creatures with different bodies, ranges of spiritual evolution and technological capabilities. The primary distinction seems to be that there are those who remain anchored to a physical body and those who have advanced beyond the need for a material container. The latter are more like pure energy, an intelligent light that can assume a humanoid shape if it so chooses.

I am still learning about the diversity of other life forms. They oftentimes create an illusion to mask their appearance. As a result, we can walk away with a perception very different from what really occurred. I have a very clear memory of some situations while others remain hazy, so it's advisable to regard the information in this chapter with some circumspection. Some of my knowledge is observational, while portions are based on what other beings have told me. I have to use my intuitive guidance to determine whether I am being given information that they want me to have rather than what may be the truth. It's rather like asking someone to describe their achievements. The odds are you are going to get a glowing account rather than a critical analysis.

People have asked me what determines whether a person has contact experiences. I believe it is based on several factors: your overall receptivity, your expectations, sometimes just being in a certain place at the right time if they happen to be in the area, and specific genetic patterns in your body. Some entities have been tracking certain bloodlines almost since the beginning of life on this planet. If you happen to have been born to one of those bodies, you will have visitors who monitor you.

Names

Most of the beings in the cosmos don't use designations as we do and often choose a name just for us, so we can call them something that has meaning. The name they select can be something that strikes a familiar chord with you, such as a religious affiliation (Michael, Seth, Gabriel, Balthazor) or may be a hint about their connections to past lives on this planet.

The designation can also be based on its vibrational frequency. Words make unique sounds which are harmonic vibrational patterns when they are uttered. The reverberation that is created when we use their name can set up a certain pattern that, while unseen in our third dimension, has significance in their higher planes. A particular vibration may have the ability to reach them in a way similar to how we use a phone number to call someone. It would not be the name we utter that makes the connection but the harmonic sound affiliated with it. Some of the mysticism associated with the Qaballah and Hermetic teachings is based on this principle, as are doctrines that teach how to manifest energy into matter.

What they think of us

Many of the beings have tremendous love for us and feel much the way a parent does for a child, but not all look upon us that way. Some view us disdainfully because of our frequent disregard for each other and our planet. Our violent, warring tendencies cause them concern. Numerous alien life forms regard us as an unevolved species with potential for advanced growth. They know we can be unpredictable, have an enormous amount of variation in our spiritual awareness and possess tremendous intolerance for our own species. Our specific emotional patterning and use of free will are two characteristics that seem to differentiate us from other beings. Most other entities have our best interests at heart, but will create manipulative situations that help us evolve.

Who's out there?

Many of my memories are repressed concerning what they look like because I have spent most of my life asking that I do not recall their appearance. When I describe these other life forms, there may be inaccuracies because my recollection is cloudy. They also may have superimposed a false memory to obscure my recall of what they look like.

The beings who have bodies often resemble humans to some degree, but not always. I find it interesting that most have a head and appendages in the same place where our arms and legs are. The ones I have encountered are usually bipedal, standing upright like we do. Hands and feet can differ, I have seen a thick three-segmented cloven claw-like hand for some. There can be great variation to the skin.

Many life forms are representative of the variety of species here on Earth. For example, there are creatures with appearances that resemble reptiles, insects, cats, and birds. But then there are ones for which there are no comparison—hybrids of man and machine and those with features like nothing on Earth. These forms of consciousness are hard to describe because there just aren't any frames of reference to compare them to.

There are also self-aware life forms that simultaneously share a mutual existence in a body while having an independent life. Picture a tree with leaves that connect to branches which are part of the trunk. These creatures are distinct and aware beings but live like the leaves on a tree.

Their civilizations

Most other species have societies very different than ours. In many cases, their planets are not comprised of fragmented factions, like us. They are often cohesive planet-wide civilizations, rather than many competing countries with independent agendas. Almost always, they have well organized planning with their metropolitan creations, rather than allow them to evolve randomly. They are quite astute in regard to education, resources, dwellings, rearing of their offspring, harmony with weather and planetary conditions, etc. Most have advanced societies that work together harmoniously for survival, resources and cosmic exploration. This is not to say that there are not planets with dissenting groups who have their own ideas about how things should be done. They exist, just like there are renegade factions here on Earth, but they seem to be rare in occurrence, at least in my experience. Overall, peaceful loving beings dominate, but then again we attract experiences in accordance with our expectations. If I expected violent, dangerous entities, my consciousness would open a door that would bring this to me.

Specific voyagers have been coming from many places for a long time. Several beings have followed us for millennia, however, we have more recently attracted visitors from places that are newer to us. There is a lot going on with our evolution at the moment, and we make an interesting study for many creatures.

The Pleaidians

The Pleaidians appear to have been around us for a very long time, many thousands of years. They are humanoid, but there is something different about them. I am not sure what, I suspect most of our differences lie in physiological chemistry, rather than appearance. However, they can pass for one of us quite readily. Some of the men's ears are larger and a little lower. I recall one male had a strong hawk-nose, like an Indian or Middle Easterner, with dark straight hair; however he is one of the ancient ones who was here for the genetic alterations thousands of years ago (more about that later).

They treat us like their children and claim to have strong genetic ties to us. They can be very loving, but we are like their science project and they are studying us because of our close links. In fact, they are more than researching us; they are responsible for many events designed to move humans forward in their personal growth. I recently discovered they use androids and suspect I will find out more about this in the future. They are responsible for many of the recent ship sightings; they intentionally want to be seen to help us become aware of alien life.

The Pleiadians are very active right now with our acceleration of learning about other life in the universe. Think of a large galactic committee monitoring and meddling with our evolution, with some beings taking more active roles and responsibilities. You can say that they are one of the more diligent committee members pushing us to evolve into a higher manifestation of ourselves.

Arcturians

Arcturians are among my favorites; I understand them as if I were one of them. Others may find them condescending, but it's important to recognize that they see life differently than us. We do many foolish things on this planet that are hard to justify. They are extremely spiritually evolved, far more than most species. Their society is well thought out and extremely productive. The Arcturian regards us as very simple with odd customs, however, I know that they are somehow privy to hidden, precise information about how our evolution is scheduled to happen. They know, while others think that they know. Arcturians seem to have strong connections to multidimensionals and overlords, beings that I will explain momentarily.

A friend once described them as behaving like proper aristocratic Englishmen who are rather disdainful of American habits. They have no idea they sometimes come across as a bit arrogant; truly they mean no harm or disrespect. It is attributed to a cultural variation between our species and should not be taken personally. They just see us as not making sense a lot of the time because we can be so destructive to ourselves, our neighbors and our home planet. However, I find they have great logic.

For example, it's difficult for them to understand why we would smoke a cigarette knowing full well it may harm us physically. This type of behavior is odd to them. They also tend to use descriptions of things rather than the actual word. Instead of saying cigarette, they say, "the long cylindrical tubular shape that is lit with fire at one end and emits a pungent smoke."

They are light years ahead of us in understanding the universe, life, reality and one's relationship to the God presence. When they join with me to channel knowledge, I feel intellectually brilliant and can see answers to almost anything in the universe. They are a particularly good source for information about scientific topics like quantum physics, universal conditions and space travel.

Most of my recall of their appearance is wiped out. I have only a vague memory of what they look like and find it hard to describe because I don't have a frame of reference to compare them to. I tend to see a shorter, pudgy species and suspect they are not all that human in appearance.

Reptilian species

Reptilian species are a common visitor, at least for me. They almost always wear a uniform. One evening, five males hazily appeared in my room, arranged like a police lineup. They wanted me to see the variation among their features, so I could detect what was a consistent trait to the species and what was unique to an individual due to hereditary variation. Some had heavier rounder faces, and others were leaner with sharper, narrower features. Because of this, I am under the impression there are two primary divergences in their species. It is mostly evident by the face, characterized by either the more massive head or the thinner longer variety. They look a little human but their skin is leathery/scaly. I cannot see their hands and feet clearly.

One once appeared in my kitchen, partially cloaked between dimensions and telepathed for me to pick up paper and pen to write. I scratched out shapes that looked like elementary pictographs conveying recognizable symbols. One item looked like a round spaceship, another was a spiral denoting movement. I did not understand what he was trying to tell me, so I asked for a translation. Suddenly, I began to write under the pictures. He said that he had been given permission to meld his mind with mine before he left our planet, so he could understand the human species from my observation point. He indicated the permission came from the multi-dimensional overlords and thanked me for allowing my participation, so he could learn about us.

He noted his amazement that our "central command center" was full of "darkness and blight, while most other planets were filled with light." He was referring to our country's capitol, Washington DC. He remarked on the violent crime in the city and corruption within the institution. He found it confusing and sad.

At one time, reptilian representatives conveyed that they were the Verdean society. Their civilization emphasizes culture and educational training. This has left me a little perplexed because not long after that incident, a gentleman wrote a book about his experiences with the Verdant creatures. The names are hauntingly similar, yet his encounter was definitely not reptilian. However, I feel his account is authentic based on my own experiences. Perhaps I misunderstood the name, translated it wrong, or someone was pulling a prank giving me the wrong information. This would be like switching name tags with someone. However, I know if this was the case, there would be a reason for it that would become evident at a later date. This is a very loving society, and I do not believe the name mix-up, if there was one, would be due to misguided humor.

Zeta Reticuli (Grays)

My experiences with what people call Grays are different than most. They often regard me with friendliness and treat me well. I call them Pillsbury dough boys because of their small, rounded appearance. Their bodies are delicate and almost a translucent pasty white with a pale blue gray tinge. They have classic large, dark, almond shaped eyes that extend over much of the top of their face. I find it distracting that there is just a large dark orb with no center. Either they do not have a pupil, or I just don't recall seeing it. Like the Arcturians, their minds are very analytical, and they are researchers at heart. I have heard that there are several variations of this species that have evolved differently, some being friendlier than others. I do not have first hand information about whether that is true, but I have had experiences that might support this. A slightly darker gray variety has visited and they are more austere and lack warmth. These visits were very technical without as much consideration for me.

They have a strong group consciousness, as their minds are somehow linked. The power of their presence when they mentally touch you can be daunting. Their thoughts bear little resemblance to ours and I think that is what terrifies some people. We are not used to highly intelligent beings whose thinking processes are ordered differently. We cannot relate to them.

When they explore my body, I have always sensed the presence of a higher being guiding them, setting parameters for what they could do. It felt kind of like a guardian was there, ensuring there were no slip-ups that would render me inoperative for this life's work.

I noticed not long after one visit that I had a small bump, less than the size of a flattened pea, at the top of my head. It could be a benign fatty tumor that often appears without reason. However, I find it suspicious, since some beings implant tracking devices within our bodies. Most of these implants are biological rather than technological constructs, which allows them to remain undetected and secure for a long time.

I have been treated with increasing friendliness over the years by these beings, like a colleague. As I matured and became more spiritually aware, I was more interesting than the usual "roundup" of humans. I was someone who could understand them on different levels; they longed for me to allow conscious recall of our work together. Despite their growing warmth, I vehemently insisted upon blocking memories of my contact with all alien species.

We had an agreement that there would be no recall of their faces, but one time a lapse happened. After participating in an experiment that evaluated the potential of two opposable thumbs on each hand, I was taken to a cockpit, or central command center. As I was shown around, the veils momentarily lifted and their faces were etched clearly into my consciousness. Horrified with the impending reality of full remembrance, I screamed to have the memory covered up, to keep the incident repressed. They so deeply wanted to communicate with me, to have me take the next step of retaining full awareness of what had happened. They had the sadness of a disappointed child when I overreacted. I returned with recall of the event, along with a small scar on my right wrist underneath the thumb, where a probe had been inserted. The mark was visible for many years. To this day, I can only clearly remember the eyes of the commander looking straight at me, telepathically asking me to remember.

Andromedans

We are now having a lot of contact with Andromedans. I keep seeing a very human looking being, resembling us a bit, when I try to remember their image. They are very scientifically advanced. Many people who have a finely developed scientific or medical intellect have ties to this planetary civilization. I say this because when I meet these folks, I am telepathed about their connection to this civilization.

The Andromedans have a strong presence; it's like encountering a person whose personality floods a room when they arrive. While many beings have a sense of humor, they are pleasant but rather serious. I have seen a connection between many young Americans in their twenties and the Andromedan culture. I suspect these young adults are being groomed by representatives from this galaxy and that their generation will bring forth many significant advances in science and medicine.

Brown Humanoids

I have no idea who these beings are, but they resemble humans who have the underlying muscle tissue exposed, as if they don't have skin. Rather than the customary red coloring of muscle, they are golden brown. Their eyes are light blue and they have no hair. They said they live between our dimensions and observe us constantly. They showed me how they exist within a series of consecutive folds that look like waves of space doubled over and bent back on itself.

There seem to be countless alien life forms out there and many authors have written about their impressions of various planetary beings. Syrians, Orions, even types of androids can be found in literature. The horned bovine gods depicted in ancient Egyptian art are said to be a race called Venusian Hathors. Just as there are numerous Earth societies with people of different appearances and customs, there is intercultural variation beyond our planet. Perhaps as we discover other beings, we will finally learn to embrace our diversity, rather than judge it.

They think they know more about us than they do

Many of the entities are presumptuous about how much they think they know of us. They remind me of a primatologist who studies apes and their culture. She may observe them, live among them and love them, but she will never truly know what it is like to be one or belong to their society. Some of these extraterrestrial beings have studied us for thousands of years, but they do not understand us as much as they believe they do.

Multidimensionals

Multidimensional beings are different than the extraterrestrials, often the situations are more spiritual. Although it may be argued that any entity that can traverse dimensions is multidimensional, I am referring to some of the highest evolved forms of consciousness. They often appear in human form because they know we are most comfortable with a familiar presence. I was once told by them that the difference between an experience with a multidimensional and an ET is like "the difference between spiritual rapture and scientific inquiry." By this they meant that the ET's study us, are often technologically oriented and scientific in their objectives. The higher multidimensional experience is more like undergoing a profound spiritual event. They are bathed in powerful love that is sensed by us. They have no need of technology because they are far beyond it. These beings are gentle and at the same time, profound jokesters who love us but find us amusing.

Their humor is very slapstick, and they often use puns and riddles. They are here to teach us. Many of the ones people refer to as ascended masters are actually high multidimensionals assuming the form of an ancient, timeless teacher.

They used to appear before me as humans, but they now say I have gained enough understanding where it is no longer necessary. Instead, they look like a wave pattern of energy that comes into my sphere, then is decrypted by my consciousness. Through this method, I receive whatever information they want to impart.

There seems to be a "pecking order" among them, much like a hierarchical arrangement. Each spiritual being respects how they are intricately related as they carry different tasks but equal responsibility. I call the ones at the top Overlords because of the respect they command and the influence they carry. There is one being I have met who seems to be at the upper echelons of these creations in consciousness. He is called Melchizedek.

Meeting Mel

I used to find myself saying, "Yes, Mi'lord" to someone when I was quite young. I did not know who Mi'lord was, until he revealed his identity when I was in my late thirties. I had spoken to him throughout my life and when he appeared I had always felt as if I was "reporting in." It seemed as if he was checking on me to evaluate my progress here.

I learned more about him one day while resting on my couch. Suddenly, I saw his image. I was then directed to pick up a pen and wrote "Melchizedek" followed by another name. He telepathed that the first name was his, and the second was my spiritual name. It was instantaneously communicated that this was who I had been talking to all my life. I did not know anything about him or his name, except I thought I may have heard it before and perhaps it was biblical.

Later, I asked some friends if they knew who or what Melchizedek was. No one did. Finally, someone was able to tell me that he was of the highest echelons of the White Brotherhood. I learned that this was not the hate mongering racist gang but an alleged hierarchy of enlightened entities who oversee the administration of the universe.

My first fully conscious encounter with him was different than any other prior experience. While other encounters come easily and I feel the information as it is passed along, this was not the same. The environment was filled with golden light. His presence had more power than I had ever encountered. Oddly, I seemed to be inside him, at one with his consciousness, while simultaneously standing before him somewhere in space. While all this was happening, I remained fully aware and knew that my body was still in my living room.

His voice, although silent and heard only in the inner realms, carried a power and intensity I had never before experienced. He said I was deliberately designed with aspects that were very God-like, or spiritual. He showed me that we were all his children, but there was a sequential hierarchy of awareness and some people had been seeded on Earth who were scheduled to be stronger leaders.

I was shown a visual display of dots of differing darkness and intensity. Many dots were very light speckles and too numerous to count. Strewn among these were darker spots that were less frequent. Even fewer than these were specks of the greatest intensity. All of these points represented human beings on Earth at this time.

The darkest dots were incarnated children who would act as leaders by fulfilling spiritual work to help direct the others. He then imparted a personal message about my role: I was created to serve the people of Earth. I was one of the dark dots and scheduled to fulfill a strong leadership role in my lifetime.

While some might walk away from an experience like this believing they have a special mission, I choose to just consider it with interest. Sometimes we fulfill destiny in the most mysterious and unexpected ways. What we anticipate for our lives and what comes to pass are often quite different.

These other types of life reach out to us frequently and transmit using different methods. Speech is not common among extraterrestrials. Instead, they rely on five primary ways when they make contact.

Chapter Seven

Different Species, Different Ways

Humans are accustomed to speaking aloud to communicate with each other, but most life in the universe does not indulge in this method. Instead they make use of richer processes beyond words. Most commonly interact with us through telepathy, holographic communication, altered states, implants, and experiences in shared consciousness.

One of our human distinctions is that our thoughts are translated into spoken words before they can be shared. To transmit to us through speech, ET's first enter our minds to assess the way our patterns of thinking organize themselves into sentences and entire messages. Some entities have studied us for a long time and have the mechanism for this well understood. Although most other life forms do not rely on spoken words to communicate, they generally use it when working with us because that is what we are accustomed to.

Some beings, when borrowing a human body to speak (such as in channeling), sound like a foreigner who uses incomplete sentence fragments and odd choices of words. As a result, they are difficult to understand. However, this problem usually diminishes with practice; the more that they work with us, the better they are able to familiarize themselves with our systems and manipulate the human body. As with all things, practice makes perfect.

Materializing

When contact happens, they can either come to you or bring you to them. When they arrive, the visits often happen without much warning. My psyche is shaken as it once again is confronted with the realization that the superficial life I call reality is being challenged. Generally, encounters are preceded by an alteration in perception and a vibrating noise that is more felt than it is heard. I experience it primarily in my head but also my heart region and my stomach. Then I enter into a hazy type of consciousness with modes of communication beyond what I am accustomed to.

Notice of a visit generally happens only moments before impact, though there can be times when they can be sensed even hours before contact happens. Generally, in these situations, they subtly let you know they are there and wait until you are ready for them.

The unnerving thing about ET's is that they often appear suddenly in your room at night. They like to get us while we are in a sleep state because we are more accommodating. They just don't understand that it is frightening to be aroused suddenly to face the unknown. In my situation, they wake me so I can be an active participant and have no doubts they are there.

Much of the fear associated with encounters is actually due to the uncertainty of what is happening to us. They sneak up on us, don't reveal themselves and worse, usually enter when it is late and we are sleeping. Humans do not like to be vulnerable, and that is the situation we often face.

Telepathy

They often communicate with us through telepathy. We hear actual words, except the voice is within our head. Some beings are capable of going within our minds and replicating the exact voice patterns of people we know. They can be absolute masters at voice mimicry. This serves a purpose—sometimes it alleviates our anxiety if we think it's dead uncle Jed speaking rather than a foreign life form. We may be more apt to listen to what uncle Jed has to say, rather than heed an unfamiliar being.

Is this manipulation? Absolutely, but it's not malevolent. Often, they want to contact us and will use whatever way works. Most beings know humans get spooked by the idea of confronting alien life forms. They don't want to scare us.

Many of them are quite attached to us and try to help in ways that do not interfere with our choices of free will. Think about watching your beloved pet dog from afar as he wanders around. You cannot call out to him. You can see him, but he can't see or hear you. You want to help him find his way safely home, but you can't interfere. Now, imagine that you could gently influence his thought processes to guide him down the right street and to stay out of traffic. In many ways, we are like their pets who are the benevolent recipients of their guided thoughts. So if they can get through telepathically and perfectly replicate the sound of Uncle Jed's voice to guide you, what harm is done?

When coming through the veils of sleep, you may catch a voice teaching you. With practice, you can learn to capture the information and bring it back. The information will often be amazing. It may be related to current events or to spiritually oriented guidance.

Once I telepathically heard a woman's voice speak of changes that were about to pass on Earth. She was explaining how the wind would accelerate over certain geographic areas of the planet and begin a process of altered rain and weather patterns. It would start at the polar caps and move inward towards more central regions of the planet. It had something to do with the Earth's rotational speed changing. It was a gentle, inviting voice transmitting information. If it had been harsh and chaotic sounding, I would have ended the incident immediately due to my discomfort. I appreciate their attempts to make us more comfortable with them.

There are also beings that make clicking and popping sounds that resemble a settling house creaking. Listen closely and there is a distinct difference in the sound. Houses do not click. One time I thought, "How do you do that?" They telepathed back that they compress and shoot air, which results in the sounds we hear.

Holographic communication

One of the more common methods of communication is also how many animal species on our planet transmit information: holographic thought patterns. Holographically conveyed knowledge differs from telepathy as it involves transmission of a picture that actually is a coded symbol. Although the picture may be uncomplicated, it is accompanied by instant knowing pertaining to whatever the message is.

The information passed to us may be extensive. For example, I might suddenly see a bird's image and be shown how they communicate within their species; perceive humans; psychically transmit to us in the absence of language, and are used by forms of dimensional awareness to experience the human condition. This all occurs within a fraction of a second. It is like a computer download of an encyclopedia volume that happens in less than a moment.

Altered states

The particular hypnotic conditions they use are called fugue states. This happens when they want us to return to normal wakefulness and forget what happened but retain the information unconsciously. Apparently we have what they refer to as hidden files in our mind, the way a computer has hidden files in its system. These "files" are brought up, or activated, when they interact with us. We then enter a fugue state and are programmed with information. When they are done, the files are brought down and stashed somewhere in the mind once more. We forget about what has happened until we are once again activated. I suspect that this equivalent to a computer file is made up of a complex of nerve cells that take on an undetected function we have yet to discover.

They have demonstrated this fugue state for me. One night I was directed to my balcony. Suddenly, I entered two simultaneous states of consciousness. One half of my mind was fully aware, the other half entered into a semi-conscious, almost robotic state. It was fascinating. I have no idea how it was done. I can't help but wonder if they were able to activate the brain hemispheres separately and somehow disable the corpus collosum, the structure that connects the two halves and allows them to work in synchronicity. It was a fascinating way to demonstrate different conditions of awareness. It was also very effective and enabled me to understand in a way that exceeded any description I could have encountered.

These altered states can be lighter hypnotic or deeper trance patterns. Often, they take us out when we are in the midst of sleep. When you find yourself strangely waking up at different times during the night, it's frequently because you are being sent back to help you remember what just happened. Generally, it's pretty important information if they bring you back. It's advisable to immediately make a record of whatever you can recall.

Implants

Information can be given to us and timed for release at a later date. The trigger can be anything from meeting an unwitting person to a random event. You can have your memory activated by an encounter with someone, a whiff of a fragrance, or a simple weather condition like a storm. A TV show or a song can even bring forth the information.

As mentioned in an earlier chapter, when they embed information it can be associated with a fearful event. Your apprehension marks the incident, so it stands out in your memories. The emotion acts like a bookmark to keep it from being buried along with all the other data in your mind. We have a natural tendency to return to troubled circumstances to try to turn it into something comfortable and familiar. Because of this, your reasoning intermittently returns to explore what happened and eventually pulls out the information put there for later release.

This technique acts like a time capsule liberated only when our consciousness acknowledges we are emotionally safe and can handle the recall. Although extraterrestrials may seem callous using methods like this that are based in fear, they work. These beings do not understand humans, and they see no harm in this method that is effective.

Shared consciousness

Finally, there are shared consciousness experiences. Our encounters can be collectively perceived by other entities in a most unique manner. They attach themselves to our mind by co-habitating our bodies without our knowing this is happening. They then learn through our eyes while we remain unaware we have a hitchhiker. They are like a silent spectator who feels our responses to situations. At one level, they are gathering data about our social processes, but they are also picking up human emotional patterning.

Think about how a bacteria may stay in your body without your ever knowing it. We remain oblivious to many microbial entities that reside in us unless they become disruptive to our normal status. It's only when we develop physical symptoms that interfere with our daily activities that we become aware we may have an intrusive bacillus. Most people never know they have another life form present, just as they are often unaware of the diseases they may carry within their body.

The foreign entity is often a representative from an alien civilization who has been studying you. Generally it is present only for a short time to experience a particular situation. Certain experiences are quite unfamiliar to them in their particular existences. Most life forms do not have our range of feelings and desire to learn about our human emotion which is so foreign to many of them. If they share your consciousness, they can feel and learn as you do. Although you may not be aware of it, you have given your permission from your higher self to participate in this condition. It is a very kind, benevolent gesture that allows others to learn about the uniqueness of being human.

Because people are unaware this can and does happen, they ignore the signs and continue on normally, unaware they are transmitting information to civilizations. However, you can learn to become sensitive to the clues they are there. When I experience this, it feels like someone else is looking out through my eyes and I become aware of their impressions and thought patterns, as if they are my own.

Once, I felt my hands raise in the air until they were before my eyes. I watched as they were rotated and studied. My fingers wiggled and I heard someone disdainfully sniff, "These things are just like spiders!" as they noted that the fingers attached to our hand are similar to legs on a spider's body.

Using technology to communicate

Some species rely on technology to communicate. Some of the processes they use are similar to techniques effectively used for adult learning. They may have us view an event on a simulated screen as if it were a movie or watch a three dimensional hologram unfold in the air. Other times you may be seated in front of what appears to be a television screen and watch their version of "This is Your Life." Some will even suspend documents with written information on their ship's walls, similar to posting flipchart information about a conference room to help participants remember key points of a presentation. The images can be reviewed as if you were reading a book. The writing may be remembered as just odd symbols or read like a language.

There are alien visitors who, while in their ships, will lock onto your consciousness. You can feel this quite plainly. Generally, these are smaller crafts, but not always. They will track us, almost like an animal is monitored through the use of an implanted device that transmits their location.

You can feel it when they find you. My experience is that it has always been friendly, and they respond to my emotional state. One night I received a telepathic message to go onto my balcony. In the distance was a small ship very different than a plane or helicopter. It was round with a large front window that had a tremendous light that beamed forward and lit up the area. As I stood there amazed, it responded to my emotions, as if it were reading my mind. As it progressed toward me, I thought that I wanted it to go away. It stopped immediately and hovered, waiting for me to give my consent to come forward. Finally it flew over my house and off into the distance.

Often, they will make contact in the late night or early morning hours. This is because it's easier for them to get through. There appears to be less interfering activity that obstructs their messages, and their transmission signals can more readily penetrate. Also, most humans are sleeping at this time and thus are in a vulnerable state of receptivity.

Homework

They often leave hints after an encounter. Sometimes they teach me about a particular topic and I may think I have gained full understanding, but then later they bring another source of information into my path that reveals much more. They will impulse me to go somewhere, such as a bookstore, direct me to the proper section, then have a book glow on the shelf so I can find it. This has been important because I generally don't accept what I have been taught until I find it validated elsewhere. Discovering principles in science and physics that corroborate what they say have been helpful and were influential in my agreeing to come forward to tell of my experiences.

Problems with communication

Translation errors

It's crucial to be aware of problems that can occur when communicating with other life forms. Most people aren't aware that translation errors can happen. I was taught about this in a fascinating way. I was in a ship and suddenly everything began to change and become distorted. The walls moved in and out, while senseless utterances were heard in the air. This demonstration was to show me how the walls' movement and the miscellaneous sounds were no more than meaningless artifact, a byproduct of "fine tuning" while they were finding the right frequency to transmit. It was like extraneous static on a transmission line. Someone unaware of this might return to Earth feeling they had just undergone a very significant event, when it actually was inconsequential. We have to be discretionary, so we don't misinterpret something meaningless as something profound.

Manipulation

As I mentioned earlier, we can be readily manipulated. Therefore, we must carefully evaluate everything we are told. Many species will claim to be the "most advanced in the universe." How are we to know any better? They will also frequently try to convince you that you are special and have a mission of importance for the fate of the Earth. This may be flattering but decide carefully about your actions and acceptance of tasks. Just because you are communicating with someone not human does not mean your discretion should go out the window. If you met a group on the subway who convinced you they were part of a new organization to save the Earth and its inhabitants, would you necessarily abandon your life and join them?

During one of the most significant visits of my existence, I was requested to come publicly forward and discuss what I know about interactions with other life forms. I waited a year and a half before I decided to comply. It was a decision I was not taking lightly. I needed to see proof that the world was ready for this. I was not about to trash professional and personal credibility. I wanted to ensure there would be an audience who wanted the information as I had no intention of thrusting it down anyone's throat so I could feel I did my job.

Illusion

Many entities can create masterful illusions that make them and circumstances appear differently than they are, allowing them to effectively mislead us. They are capable of creating circumstances of biblical proportion such as an image of the Virgin Mary or a bleeding stigmata to convince you to fulfill a mission. They are able to create situations that match any religious convictions you may have.

They can also put you in the midst of a seemingly real scenario that is no more than a hologram. Many species are able to bring forth this simulation without technology. They use their minds to create an illusion. The guise is controlled by the being's decisions of what should be presented. You may think you had an encounter with a very attractive human representative in a pleasant environment, but it was no more than a facade designed to make you feel comfortable.

They can also emulate other species to avoid blame for some of their activities. What if you took Sally's clothes, changed your hair to look like her and then masqueraded perfectly as her to shoplift. Poor Sally! Only now suppose rather than disguise yourself through a costume, you are able to create a perfect illusion. Some creatures can change their image completely by manipulating our perceptions of what we thought we saw. I am not so sure that certain species don't leave misleading telltale markers after abduction incidents. Because of this, I suspect some beings get blamed for other creature's activities. I think the reason for this is to preserve a stainless image for when they finally integrate more openly with our society. We will be more likely to trust representatives from a civilization that we don't blame for manipulating us in the past.

Where are they?

So where are these beings when they communicate with us? Why can't we see them? They reside in a variation of time and space that is very close to here. They can see us at all times and also hear our thoughts. Often, if you pay attention, they will communicate with you. They are in a slightly parallel existence that is like being separated by the skin of a balloon. It's similar to a one-way mirror and we are on the blind end. It is here that beings cloak themselves and walk around us.

They can slip into our realm on a frequency that enables them to be invisible to us. Our time space location is actually a coordinate that can be keyed into the cosmos. It is a lengthy numerical formula. If you vary the end numbers by one or two digits, you end up right near where you want to be but remain cloaked by a thin veil. This "subsequencing variation" is where they reside. There are portals and wormholes along the way that can be inserted as part of the equation (in the form of a numerical equivalent) to get one to their destination more quickly.[16]

There are two other considerations critical to understanding our relationship to them and how they can do the things they do. One concerns the nature of reality and the other is genetics. First, let's look at what we do and don't know about our reality.

---

16 This is somewhat similar to how hyperlinks are used in cyberspace. The hyperlink is a lengthy character sequence that identifies a (cyber) location. It can be used as a shortcut to get from one location to another.

CHAPTER EIGHT

THE NATURE OF REALITY
(GOD'S OWN MOVIE THEATER)

The UFO and extraterrestrial phenomena is not about little gray men or different life forms. It is about understanding the marriage of consciousness and science. It's about learning how unknown universal principles can explain what is thought to be impossible. Most importantly, it's about our human spiritual evolution and relationship to a higher consciousness.

In our pursuit to understand reality and consciousness, we have taken two different tracks. One is the way of the scientist, who requires measurable data and concrete evidence to quantify an event. The other path is the way of the mystic, who chooses to blithely accept experience and just know. Perhaps it's time to quantify the mystical by extracting the best from the scientist and the spiritualist. In some ways, we have begun to do this within quantum physics. It was here that I discovered parallels to my teachings that allowed my scientific mind to embrace the seemingly impossible suggestions they made about the true nature of reality.

As we prepare to come into increased contact with other beings, we will need to understand as much as possible to meet them on their level. By learning about the deception of time, reality and creation, we can begin to fathom the mysteries they already know.

The following passages share some ideologies from the other species, along with a little science relevant to their teachings. I am not saying that the contents within this chapter are absolute truth, that is for each reader to decide. The teachers who have worked with me have made sure that I understand that there is no one singular version of truth because as something is thought, so it becomes. Something imagined is as concrete as something real. There are only infinite possibilities comprised of endless pathways.

Differences in realities

Other realities are very distinct from ours and not confined by the parameters that govern here. Consciousness operates under different guidelines, and thoughts that might seem bizarre in this world make perfect sense in other realms. Distorted thinking is accepted as reasonable, and things that have order here are random there. Day and night are not applicable, our social rules have no meaning, and laws of mechanical physics don't apply.

Our linear model of time seems to have no significance outside our domain. Fifteen hundred years may translate as nine minutes from one environment to another. Conversely, we can believe we have been away the duration of lifetimes to find we were gone only a few hours. In other settings, we might stay in one place, such as a room in a house, for the equivalent of centuries because we focus only on the moment at hand. The trick is to avoid getting caught in illusory time traps by empowering ourselves to gain self-awareness as we travel the cosmos. Attaining this independence is contingent on understanding about the mystery of dimensions and time-space.

Dimensional physics theories

The idea we live within many dimensions is a favorite notion in both mainstream thought and modern physics. The multiple dimension premise is important because it helps us grasp multidimensional reality and understand how the cosmos is tied to other realms.

One of the more common proposals is hyperspace theory, often talked about with the superstring theory, which suggests that all matter can be reduced to very small strings of energy that vibrate within a universe. The reason the hyperspace premise is so important is that many physics theories that had glitches suddenly become theoretically operable when applied in the higher dimensions of hyperspace.

Hyperspace focuses on the idea that our universe originally existed within ten dimensions, but at one point, it became unstable and cracked into two parts. The first component is comprised of the first four dimensions.[17] The other six dimensions fissured down to a size smaller than an atom but exist within their own construct of time and space. Some scientists have wondered if we could jump into these other spaces to save ourselves if we destroy our living quarters here. Another similar idea suggests that universes are like bubbles that pop in and out of dimensions while souls flit from universe to universe. Death is merely a transition to a new place as beings jump from one world to another.

Each domain has its own set of rules that makes sense to its inhabitants but can be confusing or nonsensical to an outsider. By gaining knowledge about the true nature of the cosmos, we can gain better understanding of each different reality. If we momentarily step outside our viewpoint, we can more readily grasp other dimensions and the life forms anchored to each one.

Flatlanders, us and higher dimensionals

We don't understand the mystery of how higher dimensional beings operate because we have yet to learn what they already know. Our simple and limited understanding of these creatures can be readily forgiven when we look at the analogy of how two dimensional beings regard us.

The nineteenth century mathematician Carl Gauss first introduced the concept of Flatlanders to demonstrate how individuals in different dimensions might regard each other. A Flatlander is a two dimensional creature that resembles a flat stick figure sketched on a piece of paper. If you draw a circle around him, he regards it as an impenetrable barrier. Unable to see beyond this false boundary, he remains stuck, trapped in a prison comprised of his own dogmatic illusions. If one of us, a three dimensional entity, were to come along and lift him over the circle to freedom, he would see it as a miracle and regard us as a god. Our response would be to gently smile at his naivete because we see and know more than he does about the true nature of his reality.

---

17 We reside in the third level.

Consequently, when a higher entity comes into our third dimension, he has knowledge of things we have yet to learn. He warps dimensions, navigates wormholes and travels through space. Cloaking between dimensions is commonplace and dematerializing is a mundane act. When he suddenly passes through a solid wall and materializes, he appears to come out of nowhere. His appearing and disappearing is as fundamental to him as is our getting into a car and driving to a destination, yet we find his actions confounding because we don't know how he does it. We are as innocent as the Flatlanders when it comes to understanding higher dimensionals.

The Others say that we are about to uncover new material that will change the way we view life. We are getting ready to enter a new era based on a fresh understanding of physics. Apparently this information has always been here, but we weren't ready to see it. If something does not make sense, we frequently dismiss it or consider it an unexplained miracle, just like the Flatlander. As a result, we tend to overlook answers that lie in front of us.

Dimensions influence each other

There are numerous dimensions that are not separate but remain linked to each other. Because of this connection, an event in one will have a rippling effect on another. By virtue of this interconnectedness, we can enter other realities and accomplish things that will influence our existence. This has great significance because it gives us the power to affect our future and even change our past.

Conventional physics claims it is impossible to change the past, but I have been taught by the Others that it changes constantly. These other beings say that the reason we cannot return to the past is because it ceases to exist once it happens. We remain blissfully unaware of this phenomenon and conform our consciousness to adapt to whatever reality is presented to us at the moment. This is quite a provocative suggestion; it means that the Civil War might have been lost by the North, Hitler may never have initiated World War II and John F. Kennedy may not have been assassinated in Dallas one history-changing day. Ludicrous? Perhaps, but how would we know differently if we were programmed to accommodate to a reality that, unbeknownst to us, was changing all the time? To repeat the quote of higher visitors presented earlier:

> *What was once, is no more. As we travel the path of knowledge, learning and what you perceive as time, instances continue to change... the dramas and situations have changed due to the influence of present, current and even future events upon those paths so things will never be the same.*

Nuclear power and consequences on reality

It is this connection to other planes that explains why some beings are concerned about our access to nuclear power. If we act irresponsibly and bring about wide-spread destruction, it will have consequences in other time-space locations because many dimensions are connected to each other.

They have tried to convey the seriousness of irresponsible handling of destructive nuclear forces by guiding me to a place in the cosmos where there was a noticeable void. A planet with a flourishing civilization was once located there, but it was now gone. A recording of a voice played over and over again; the message was from a tribunal demanding that the accountable beings who destroyed the planet return and take responsibility for their actions. I could perceive a halo imprint in the ethers that revealed what happened. It read like a record, only it was fading. It seemed there had been a hostile action taken by marauders who used nuclear forces to detonate the planet. I am unsure why I encountered this experience but suspect it was because they are very concerned about our use of nuclear weapons. I think they wanted me to see the potential consequences of reckless actions. If dimensions are linked, then we will influence far more than our own fate if we take a rash action.

Boundaries overlap

The Others claim that we don't yet understand the universe because we revert to thinking in two and three dimensional perspectives. The ends to universes are not straight, curved or jagged. Instead, they merge into each other in multiple dimensions. Some places where universes overlap look almost like bubbles dribbling into a larger field.

I was shown a picture of a sandy beach to help me understand what they were trying to convey. In the sand, small tunnels of varying sizes and widths had been burrowed. As the water began to fill the holes in the beach, they said that is how the universes join. They are pegged together but in the way that water fills a hole in the sand. These points of connectedness have great potential; you can enter other frequencies with ease and readily cross into other realities at these sites.

Demonstrating dimensional crossover

The Others had me undergo their version of a field experiment to demonstrate the effect of dimensions shearing into one another. Unaware that anything unordinary was about to happen, I approached my home thermostat and watched my hand and part of my arm disappear as I reached up to change the temperature setting. I quickly withdrew, thinking I imagined it. As I tried it again, the same thing happened. Amazed, I pulled my arm back and forth several times and watched it dissolve in front of me on each pass.

My arm did not go through the wall, although it appeared to do so. I suspect the others changed the frequency of the vibration at that site so when I encountered that spot, it appeared as if my hand went through the solid wall.

Archetypal Consciousness

Beyond the role of dimensions, they have brought forth another startling premise to help us understand who we are. This is the role of a primary consciousness that replicates itself throughout the echoes of different universes and from which all humanoid life is based.

The Others say that we are actually extensions of very highly evolved streams of self-aware life. These beings are conscious, active and appear as a wave formation. They are living light, the caretakers of creation and close to primordial God consciousness. I have been told that our existence here is an illusion, like an animation, projected onto the landscape of this planet, directed by these higher beings. We are their thought projections that enable them to experience emotion and life in a physical body through our experiences.

These primal sources have several basic archetypes from which all human life is modeled; we are derived from these predominant thought patterns that predate our universe. There are limited models that can be varied in an endless number of combinations. This process is similar to how DNA uses restricted amounts of raw materials to create infinite life forms (this is covered in the next chapter). Our DNA is actually a model that imitates this consciousness' replication process. While the archetype creates non-physical life, the DNA method manufactures a material form that can assume consciousness.

When you discover how to recognize the archetypal origins of a person, you can map the tendencies their life will take because these basic models carry patterns for behavior. This is how I am often able to anticipate what will happen in a person's life. I read their primal codes.

These archetypal beings are connected to us through an awareness comprised of our sum total existence. This link between us is called an oversoul.

The oversoul

Early in my life, they awakened my realization of other incarnations to get me ready for the idea of the oversoul, which is a higher evolved version of ourselves. This advanced aspect helps to direct all our incarnated lives. Our multiple existences are coordinated by this oversoul who provides unseen guidance. It is like the hub of a wheel and our many lives are the spokes leading to it.

They spent years helping me to understand this concept. I initially rejected it because I could not fathom that I was comprised of more than my current existence. I had a body and as far as I was concerned, that was all there was of me. I soon learned that we are many aspects of connected awareness that ultimately lead back to a primordial consciousness. The situations I have undergone helped me understand how I can be a part of something more. I am like the finger to the hand, which is part of the arm, which is in turn connected to a larger unit called a body. The body is part of an even greater model comprised of many beings who make up a society. Spiritually we are linked ranges of consciousness that can flow back and forth to each other while remaining organized by the oversoul.

Comparing us to film actors

In an attempt to convey the convincing illusion of our reality, my teachers compare our existence to movie films. They say our sojourn here is like the movie goer who voluntarily suspends reality for several hours to experience a film's plot. They laugh at us in a good hearted way by saying we are as deluded as a film character who believes she is separate from the actress who plays her. The only difference between us and the screen character is that she is in a two-dimensional world, while we reside in three. Just like the actress' creation, we believe we are real, materially dense and separate from our source when we are actually illusions made of vibrations, powered by aware light. We are conscious holograms.

The Others showed me that the oversoul is to us as the actress is to the character. The oversoul is the master coordinator of all the lives, while the actress is the link for the many parts she has played. "Which is more real?" they asked me, "the character in a screenplay or the private life of the actress?"

The character is a celluloid imprint on a film, brought to "life" by a light shone through a projector. She has emotions, feelings and is self aware. She accepts everything in the script as her real life as do those around her, unaware that her existence is just an illusion. Whether the setting is ancient Babylon, medieval France or the contemporary United States, the character is confined to the social rules of that period, just as we must face the consequences of the society in which we live.

Like the actress' connection to the character, the oversoul is part of us. It "looks out" in an oversight capacity and is a common thread of awareness that we share with all of our other lives. The oversoul knows how things are supposed to turn out because it is aware of the details of each thoughtfully planned existence, just like an actress knows what is in the script. Unseen and unrecognized, the oversoul guides each incarnated life and offers beneficial direction. At the completion of our lives we evaluate how we did along with our oversoul, just as the actress appraises her portrayal of the character. Performing well in real life might constitute showing unconditional love, facing adversity with integrity and honesty, overcoming a drug habit, or other hardship. We may not get an academy award, but we will gain access to more complex opportunities to help us grow. As a part of an intricate group awareness, we build on our communal learning experiences.

Along with learning about how our consciousness experiences life in the third dimension, our bodies hold certain keys to our fuller cosmic identity. We have only modest understanding of how our genetic code works. DNA holds a large piece of the mystery to unraveling our full identity.

Chapter Nine

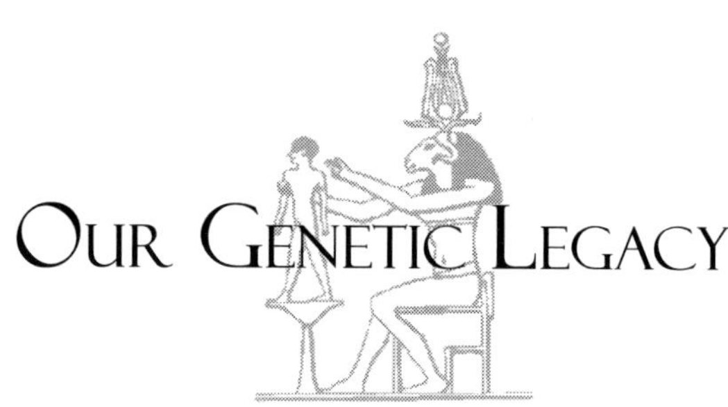

Our Genetic Legacy

Just what is the connection between our physical bodies and who we are? It appears there is a vast amount of information about our origination on this planet, our genetic codes and our unfolding destiny.

The Others have taught me about many things, but one of the more controversial concerns who they say we truly are as a species. They claim that man was a genetically manipulated experiment who evolved far beyond everyone's wildest dreams. Originally created by an oversight species that required workers, they claim that twelve different alien races were used to create our unique genetic template.

They directed me to the work of a scholar named Zecharia Sitchin. I was not sure who he was, but awoke one morning to hear them chanting his name, over and over again. When I opened up a newspaper during breakfast, it fell open to a large advertisement for an upcoming local seminar of his. I attended and was introduced to his work.

Zecharia Sitchin, I discovered, is a highly educated scholar who is one of a handful of people who can translate the ancient Sumerian language. Historically considered to be a birthplace of civilization, archeological expeditions have unearthed clay tablets engraved with numerous stories detailing Sumer's history. Mr. Sitchin has translated these writings and documented his observations in a series of books called the *Earth Chronicles.*

These publications share his conclusions about the numerous references to a city named Ur that tells of visiting "gods" from another planet who interfered with man's natural evolution on Earth.

These advanced beings, according to the ancient stories, came to Earth with a quest to mine precious materials needed for their home planet. Their own work crew became disenchanted with the circumstances here, revolted and a race of worker beings was created from a genetically altered earth creature designed to fulfill their needs. They subsequently manipulated this primitive being for their own purpose and led him to believe that they were gods.

Interestingly, in one of the channeled rhymes that alleges we are a created species, they make reference to Mr. Sitchin by name, claiming he is very close to being accurate with his theory that extraterrestrials were the early "gods" and that man was genetically manipulated to serve their needs. They say he "is close but wrong." (That channeling, *The Truth is Upon Us*, is included in the second section of this book. What is supposed to be incorrect with his proposal is discussed later in this chapter.)

This concept of genetic tinkering, proposed by the aliens, Mr. Sitchin and others, may not be that farfetched. There are oddities about our genetic code and other aspects of our physiology that to date, have never been explained satisfactorily.

Our genetic code

Our genetic code is made up of something called deoxyribonucleic acid, commonly called DNA. Essentially it acts as the written directions that tells everything in your body what to do and how to do it. It directs our cells to make amino acids that produce proteins, which in turn make all our organs and tissues.

Everything that happens in our bodies is linked to the directions that come from our DNA codes. It is responsible for the way we look and how we often behave. It is the reason why some people have blue eyes and others brown, why some people are blonde and others brunette, why some have black skin and others have white. Baldness, disease, dietary preferences, learning capabilities, all have genetic ties.

Its structure

What is most interesting about our genetic code is its structure. DNA is made of two strands of genetic material that wrap around each other in what is called a double helix. In between these strands are molecules called nucleic acids (or bases) that reach across the two strands like rungs on a ladder. There are only four types of these bases and they combine themselves in groupings of three, to make a set. Each of these sets of triplet sequences make a code to produce an amino acid that gives specific directions to each cell. As many as six different combinations can make the same amino acid and there are three codes that do not produce any amino acids; these are essentially "turned off."

Interestingly, if we include the three turned off codes there are sixty-four mathematically possible combinations to create amino acids, yet our body makes only twenty different ones. Another unique feature about our human genetics is that approximately only three percent of the DNA in our bodies is used for coding functions. The remaining ninety-seven percent appears to be untouched; we have yet to figure out why it is there.

Limitations

There are some interesting things to consider about our DNA. For example, there are only two strands of genetic material that wrap around each other. Why two? Why not four, five, ten, twelve or more? And why are there only four nucleic acids available to combine with each other? Why do these nucleic acids bind together only in groups of three? Why is the code read only in one direction? Why are three sequences turned off so they don't code for any amino acids? Why are we making less than one-third of the possibilities for amino acids? Why do we use only three percent of the entire genetic material available to us? It's almost as if someone sold us a model that is not functioning at full capacity. It could be argued that maybe it did not come with all of the features activated.

Molecular chirality

There's one other strong peculiarity. Scientists are now hotly pursuing a path to learn more about our genetic makeup and molecular chirality.

Some types of molecules come in pairs that are mirror images of each other. They resemble matched gloves that have a right and left hand: they look alike when they face each other but if you hold them side-by-side you can see that they have parts that face different directions. This right and left mirror imaging is called chirality.

Scientists conducting lab experiments found there should be an equal number of these left and right-handed molecules when they are randomly produced in a lab setting. But on Earth, all life is made from amino acids that are left-handed and sugars in the genetic code that are right-handed[18]. This consistent handedness is referred to as homochirality.

The biggest question they are trying to unravel in this situation is how homochirality came about on Earth and why the amino acids are left-hand predominate rather than right. Could this be random or was there an influencing factor?

Recent evidence is raising suspicions that the influence could have come from the cosmos. A tested piece of meteorite was found to have amino acids with only left-handed chirality, leading some scientists to believe this biological curiosity has its origins in outer space.

Mutation

There are just a few known ways to bring about changes to the DNA structure: spontaneous random mistakes that happen during replication stages; chemical processes; temperature differences and radiation. It's this last catalyst that seems to hold a key to our destiny. There is something rather interesting occurring in the universe right now that affects genetic mutation.

The past thirty years have witnessed unexplained incidents of interstellar radiation, with a marked increase in activity since 1991. Most recently, mysterious radiation bursts have been noted in nearby galaxies, particularly within the Orion Nebula. During December of 1997, the largest known explosion in the cosmos was recorded; scientists think it may possibly have heralded the formation of a new galaxy back in time. Because of how long it takes for light to reach us, we may just now have become aware of an event that happened as long ago as twelve billion years.

There is something very interesting about these recent radiation bursts that may tie into future mutations. The recent gamma ray activity,

18 Left handed sugars do exist by they are rare.

particularly from the Orion constellation, has been found to be circularly polarized. This means that its rays resemble corkscrews. If radiation happens to be circularly polarized, as in the case of the Orion source, then it breaks down genetic material based on if it is right or left handed. The determination of the right or left choice is based on the direction of the radiation's corkscrew rotation.

This means that this new source of radiation could have either of two effects, depending on whether it selects for the right or left handed chirality of our genetic molecules. It could have no influence, or we could be facing very significant mutational and evolutionary changes. This increase in polarized radiation is happening at a time when we have destroyed a large part of our natural shield against cosmic radiation: the ozone layer. Could this be coincidence? I don't think so, based on what the Others have told me.

How this ties in with what they taught me

I came upon the above research findings after I had been told by the Others that we are evolving past our current DNA structure. This is one of the times when they provided me information, then subsequently guided me to scientific data that correlated with what they said. It is up to each person to decide whether he or she believes the following scenario. If it is true, the implications for us are tremendous.

They say we are in the midst of a significant evolution to our species. Initially, I thought we were undergoing a growth in consciousness but was soon corrected by the Others. Apparently physiological changes are about to become evident in blood and other laboratory samples as they are taken during the course of people's physical exams. They say that our scientists in the medical fields will slowly begin to notice small genetic aberrations within our population. Ultimately, these seemingly random patterns will pop up with alarming frequency. At that time, researchers will become aware that something is going on of an apparent evolutionary nature.

Many people have made nonscientific claims that man is about to evolve from a two strand to a twelve strand DNA model. Although this may be true, this is not quite what my galactic teachers have shared. The Others told me they are working on a twenty strand DNA model for a new breed of Homo Sapiens that will eventually be seeded on another planet to continue life. They say that the above radiation activity is not random, but is part of an organized process to help our species evolve.

They revealed that the cosmic radiation patterns that have been released throughout the universe are a trigger to launch a new tide of evolution by activating mutational processes. It will penetrate our bodies, reach our cells and stimulate aspects of the DNA to bring forth physiological changes. These new codes will unleash previously unavailable capabilities.

Our consciousness will migrate to another level as we integrate new ways of understanding information into our lives. Some people are already responding and having new insights, although there are many who notice no difference. Because of this, we are beginning to see a bifurcation of our society that is evidenced by changing attitudes from those who are waking up from the illusions that have held us captive for so long. According to my teachers, we are tied to a cosmic time clock, based in another galaxy, that has gone off.

They say we must realize that this activity is about birth, not death. Our planet has a consciousness we should respect, even if we do not understand it. Earth is not only an aware organism but is also pregnant. She will split into two parallel worlds. One will continue on as is, with potential geologic changes. The other will go to a higher octave vibrationally. Consciousness will be experienced in a new way: our social order will be different and many of the existing governing processes will be abandoned in favor of new governance.

The people who stay in the former vibration will be reprogrammed by a magnetic field change that will encompass the Earth. There will be hazy, confused memories and they may on occasion realize things are different, but will quickly adapt to the norm like a person with amnesia. Many of Earth's inhabitants will be gone and presumed dead.

Many people have predicted dramatic changes, including Earth upheavals and nuclear holocaust. Others believe we will have a utopian outcome. On one occasion, I asked my teachers what was planned for our destiny. They informed me that every single conceived scenario will come to pass in different parallel realities. These two situations, infinite parallel realities and the Earth shearing into two dimensions, seem like they could be in conflict with each other, but I believe the first account was addressing specific aspects of the larger situation.

The above information is why they are adamant that we must realize we can control whatever reality comes our way. We are not to dwell on catastrophic Earth changes and economic demise; if we do, we will draw these things to us. If we stay conscious and guide our thoughts, they will catapult us into a desirable reality and we will have controlled our destiny. We are like cartoon characters who must demand the pencil and draw our own comic strip.

Is this interference?

These events of cosmic radiation, mutation and growth into a different dimension are being directed by conscious higher dimensional forces we have yet to learn about. We may feel uncomfortable with other beings influencing our destiny, yet we do things of an evolutionary nature to unsuspecting creatures all the time.

Imagine a pride of lions on the Serengeti Plains where we have been able to track their evolution undetected. Suppose we discovered a weakened mating trait that could affect their continued survival and decided to expose their favorite watering spot to a bacterial microbe that could work its way into their body through ingestion. This microbe, ineffectual for other species, was able to stimulate activity to counteract a condition causing weakened embryos, thus the species' survival would be more likely.

Who decides what is barbaric and what is productive research? Why should we deem it all right to intervene in other species' destinies and then be surprised that someone may be tinkering with us? What the Others are doing is similar to this type of intervention. They are working to improve our long-term survival potential.

Science continues to unravel our history

Interestingly, recent scientific advances have revealed new information to erode some of our prior presumptions about our evolutionary tree. In 1997, it was discovered that Neandertal man, previously believed to be an evolutionary ancestor, actually had no human DNA in his structure. Laboratory testing of specimens showed no genetic ties to us, contradicting prior beliefs of ancestry. Where did he come from and where did he go? Could the Neandertal have been a parallel experiment conducted by the off-planetary races and abandoned in favor of more promising life forms that led to our current bodies? I suspect there were many variations of genetically engineered human beings along the way, many of whom have left no clues behind to reveal they existed.

Physiological hints about space derivations

Now let's look at what the aliens claim in regard to who we are. They say we are a life form based on a genetic template derived from combining twelve extraterrestrial races. I believe this is one of the places where they infer Mr. Sitchin may be in error. Mr. Sitchin suggests that the Annunaki, an oversight race from space, mixed their bloodline with an early Earth primate to produce man. However, the Others reveal they used a combination of DNA from multiple species rather than one life form for the necessary ingredients to jumpstart man's evolution.

They claim that our different primary blood types (A, B, O, AB) are linked to the alien races who are our ancestors. This might account for the enigma of the RH negative blood factor that can kill an infant at birth. This odd blood incompatibility takes on significance in pregnancy. The mother's body regards her fetus as a foreign threat and develops antibodies that try to kill it. This unexplained maternal and fetal blood group incompatibility could be a legacy that still occasionally surfaces from unsuccessful extraterrestrial cross breeding attempts with humans. An ancient experiment could have unwittingly left behind a trace element that occasionally still appears in our blood typing.

The additional area they say Mr. Sitchin has missed lies in the process used to activate the DNA. The ancient Sumerian tablets read that the gods "breathed life into clay" to create man. According to the Others, this phrase refers to a process that used sonic stimulation. Certain sounds are able to propel matter to move into specific patterns.[19] They used the equivalent of an invocation to produce a harmonic effect that stimulated the different

19 The study of Cymatics, pioneered by Dr. Hans Jenny, shows how certain frequency sounds cause specific patterns to appear in matter. Substances will organize themselves into particular designs each time a certain tone is emitted.

genetic materials to merge in a cohesive medium. This new DNA incorporated many vital aspects from the contributors. It held latent capabilities from each race that could be activated at a later time. This was a critical step necessary for a life form that was made with the capability to mutate into a divine race. We were an experiment that was designed to evolve far beyond a worker race.

The holy grail bloodline

Some of us have had alien contact because they have been studying and tracking certain bloodlines for thousands of years. One of these bloodlines will be very disconcerting to some factions. It is the holy grail, the bloodline from the one historically known as Jesus Christ, who was incarnated into a body with highly unusual DNA codes. They say documents will be found that will alter our understanding of history as we know it and that we have not had an accurate account of our true past, including that particular time on Earth. Today, there are living descendants who have inherited this unique genetic legacy. These individuals often have advanced intuitive capabilities.

How ethnic races came to be

According to them, the traces of the twelve races from which we are derived are responsible for our current physical variations and explains why some people are Oriental, Black, Caucasian or of other background. Our variations relating to skin color are not from Darwinian environmental influences for natural selection. They are based on the predominance of the mixtures of the space races driving the particular body you happen to be in. Some of these DNA templates were further tweaked along the way by their genetic scientists. They say that even our climactic preferences for where we would rather live are due to the dominance of a particular species' influence within us. Those who are attracted to hot, dry climactic environments have active reptilian codes at work while those with affinity for water and ocean settings have more of an amphibian or cetacean based species.

How can we know if any of this is true?

Is all this information controversial? Absolutely. Is it true? I do not know. I have no idea whether what they suggest is accurate or if any of it is going to unfold. Only time will reveal that. My only intention is to share what I have learned and offer it for consideration.

We will each have to use our own inner wisdom to guide us in our beliefs about the origin and destiny of our species. I confess, that at this point in time, I find their proposals more convincing than the idea of Darwinian evolution;[20] however, I would certainly accept convincing evidence that would dismiss their claims.

We have had plenty of historical hypothesizing, both scientific and religious, about who we are and what our destiny is. To date, none of the accepted theories have suggested our having been birthed or subjugated by an alien species. The outrage aimed at the early proponents of Darwinism causes me to wonder how humans will react if this is true and finds its way into society. I hope we can remain open to any possibilities that present themselves and judge them on their merit. We often tend to insist that something must be ratified by conventional science before we will consider it, yet we might miss out on a lot of potential information by waiting for sanction from authoritative sources.

Genetics and our evolution are only some of the things they have shared with me. Information about technology, ancient philosophies, decoding the universe and more have been brought by them to my door.

20 To date, anthropological research has been unable to account for many unexplained gaps in evolutionary hominid development. There are periods of time when one species seems to have mysteriously disappeared while another surfaced to take its place.

Chapter Ten

You Thought You Slept At Night?

The mystery of what happens when we sleep at night has remained an enigma throughout time. Although scientists have tried to quantify this state by measuring the body's physical responses, they seem to have missed some of the dynamics that take place. While researchers chart information about stages of sleep and affiliated brain wave patterns, they have not yet deciphered the mystical side.

During slumber, we experience circumstances that seem meaningless but when properly translated, can take on great significance. Profound guidance can be accessed within other realms because different regions of consciousness are linked to our life here. When we actively use rational reasoning and direct our purpose in sleep and altered states, we can shape our destiny and influence events coming our way. This is done by learning to understand the symbols and codes that ultimately translate into affairs on Earth.

What happens

Sleep is far more than a period of temporary amnesia to help our stream of consciousness feel rested. It is quite complex, but one of its properties seems to be a plateau for time travel. Envision a spider crawling as it spins its web. Suddenly it steps off its creation and enters a zone between the silky spun filaments. Contained within these regions are states of consciousness that remain invisible to the gliding crawler when it stays on the wispy fibers. Once it leaves the web to enter these regions, it experiences another type of awareness.

Like the spider, we send out an electromagnetic energy web as we begin to fall into sleep states. Our consciousness then follows this grid. We may stay on it, or, once we reach a certain point, access portals that are sites that send us to the equivalent of the spaces between the lines. While out in other realms, we send a portion of our consciousness back to our body by a stream of thoughts that make up an invisible cord (almost like a thread of a web). This line is like a cable of energy we use to transmit back to our cells in the physical unit.

Becoming an artful navigator

When you retain awareness passing through the different stages of sleep consciousness, you can actually feel the changes as you go from one level to another. As you travel further away from our reality, it takes more powerful concentration to stay connected here. Without deliberate control, we experience dreams that seem random and nonsensical. With control, we become artful navigators who can summon information to help us grow. We can call forth the situations we need, find the answers to questions we seek, and live our lives with ordered design.

Remaining conscious and actively bringing back information for our practical use requires training. The messages brought from other places have different qualities to them dependent on where they are from. Some are symbolic and require decoding to fully understand them. Other situations are more explicit and easy to understand.

In one situation, I was put in a bed with a deadly poisonous snake at my feet about to strike me. Just before it hit, I was whisked back to my life here. Several days after, I learned that a mentally ill acquaintance had tried to harm someone and also threatened me. This was a dangerous situation, and I was being warned by those who protect and watch over me. However, many circumstances are not as readily obvious to interpret.

One time, they showed me a three dimensional grid that, when observed up close, was made up of letters and symbols. There was something of great significance about this pattern, and I could not remember very much when I came back. Through skill, I was able to replicate the scene and replay it, like a hologram. It was then that I saw this grid was a pattern used for creation in our lives, and I was being taught how to read it. It had essence codes interwoven in the design, which function similar to DNA letters. While DNA provides directions at a cellular level to create a body, essence codes guide processes that convert thoughts into three dimensional activity. The coded symbols passing through the pattern horizontally, diagonally, vertically and multidimensionally would eventually translate into events that will take place during our lives here.

Ways to master control and stay conscious while in these other planes include the use of breathing patterns, colored light, vibrational toning of sounds and conscious intentioning. This last factor involves specific messages to your higher self to program what happens to you. Those who possess high spiritual accomplishment generally don't need these training aids, but most of us require these techniques to develop self-discipline and help us reach higher states of awareness.

Translating through the veils of forgetfulness

No matter how determined one is, you cannot keep information from dissipating soon after you bring it back here. This powerful rule governs transitioning into our dimension as much as the law that the sun will melt ice on a hot day. We can no more change these rules of forgetfulness than we can will the ice to not melt. One of the powers of this illusion is that we are often seduced into not being disciplined. We strongly believe we will remember and fail to make records that will survive the transition across the veils we must pass through. Generally, cryptic messages are just enough to trigger memories of what happened. I discovered if, while in an altered state, I record notes on a small tape recorder kept under my pillow, I am able to bypass a lot of the veils of forgetfulness that descend quickly in the morning.

Nighttime lessons

While most people sleep, I have "lessons" in an altered state. I can readily cross back to my body to make a record of the information that I preserve for later study. Sometimes I receive information, other times I actually hear myself speaking of the most interesting subjects. The teachings are usually very specific. Topics often refer to things I have never heard of, speak of events that later come to pass, and offer directions of how I should conduct my life.

Often, I have doubted the truth of the contents, then later found that the information has actual merit. Names that I thought were mythical were found within the context of ancient history and past civilizations. There have been discourse about Aesculapius, a doctor referenced in Greek and Roman history; Tehuti, the Egyptian name for the legendary god Hermes Trismegistus (also know as Thoth); and Maat and Mutt, Egyptian goddesses.

I am somewhat mystified by the biblical references I encounter. I have had no formal religious instruction this lifetime and my knowledge of the Bible rates about two on a scale of one to ten. I did not know what Gethsemane was, let alone how to pronounce it correctly, much to the ghastly consternation of the person whom I asked if they knew what it meant. Names that have been assumed by spiritual visitors, such as Methuselah, Obadiah and Melchizedek, also appear to have biblical affiliations.

Enneagrams

These nighttime teachings can be quite extensive and involved. I was told by the Others to learn about Enneagrams and discovered it is a personality classification system with uncertain origins. Some claim it is an ancient Sufi teaching, other sources state it goes back way before that and is tied to the ancient mysticism of the Jewish Qaballah. It was introduced in this century by Gurdjieff and further popularized by his student Ouspensky.

The Enneagram system identifies a primary feature for each of several character types, that, if understood, can supposedly help us to grow past limiting aspects of our personalities. Although that is what I found in books, I somehow suspected there was far more to this system that I had yet to discover. They have hinted to me that it related to the coding of the universe and the symbolism of the Sephiroth, an extensive teaching found within the Qaballah. I have not pursued this further. I know when the time is right more will be revealed to me and it will be information not found in books.

Decoding molecular patterns

I am not always asleep when they call on me for a lesson. On a plane flight over Mount Shasta, I went into an altered state and saw the mountain reveal what they said was its guiding energy force. This is a pattern from a field of vibrating particles of matter. In this case, it resembled the shape of a bird rising into flight. It also represented much more: It was a powerful symbol that could provide access to wisdom lying within the heart of that mountain. In ancient times a person would concentrate in a relaxed meditative state to discover these molecular patterns. Finally, their clairvoyant vision would unleash a code, the way a key unlocks a door, to obtain entry to states of consciousness that held vast amounts of knowledge. Concentrating on the pattern in a relaxed state would divulge a kaleidoscope of information about the object in question. They have spent the recent years teaching me about these codes that are found throughout the universe.

Iridium

Some teachings hint of discoveries we have yet to make in our current lifetimes. During one nighttime encounter, I was taught about the healing properties of something called "iridium." Just before I returned to consciousness, a metallic cross was shown. It was small, like a piece of jewelry, and encrusted with purple stones that resembled amethysts. I assumed the stones were "iridium." Days after searching mineral, rock, and crystal books, the quest was abandoned. I could find no trace of iridium; therefore, I assumed it to be nonexistent.

Unexpectedly a few months later, someone showed me a piece of jewelry that looked identical to the cross shown, stones and all. Telling my memory to those present, one of the women told me that iridium is an actual substance. Later, I found out it is a metal related to platinum and osmium which is used in jewelry, aircraft and telecommunications satellites. It was not the stones I was directed to pay attention to but the metal component of the jewelry. No wonder there was no record of iridium in mineral books.

Soon after this, there was a major telecommunications satellite system installed in space that had iridium as a key part of its technology. I am suspicious that there is more to this system than it seems because of the timing of their teaching. We may not be the only ones using this satellite system.

Why me?

I wondered why they spend so much time teaching me. I was given two reasons. They appreciate that I have obtained a broad academic education and professional background, which enables me to grasp many topics. They say they like working with me because I learn quickly and am able to piece together different aspects of information to gain meaning beyond what they share at the time. They have successfully planted hints that I reconfigured for additional information after my lessons with them. I suspect by doing this they are studying the capabilities of the human intellect. However, there is another reason for their relationship with me. They say I am genetically based from an ancient lineage that carries a strong distribution of uncommon off-planetary origins.

While gaining all this experience, I have felt like a student enrolled in a universal academy on another dimension. Because they have assisted me to master so many systems here, I suspect they have later plans for me that have yet to be revealed. What they might be remains to be seen.

Chapter Eleven

Hidden Chambers And Ancient Technology

While teaching me about dimensions, reality, consciousness and genetic tinkering upon the Earth, the Others have worked hard to lay a groundwork for two more things. The first one is the relationship between the years of Akhenaton, Jesus and occurrences happening now on our planet. The second concerns how to enter concealed chambers and access hidden records from ancient monuments like the Sphinx and pyramids. Some of this information came through in coded rhymes after rather odd mystical events. The channelings, *Riddle for Thee* and *The Heart of the Lion*, in the *Tablet Rhymes* section of this book, are just two examples of information that followed their training sessions.

Four odd, yet related, situations came about to connect these incidents together. They had me go through a setting in another state of reality with people whom I actually met in real life soon afterwards. Then they sent me to an event to trigger my recall about teachings of initiation rites from a time long ago. After my memories were refreshed, I brought forth a channeled session that spoke of the time of Aton, the sun god of ancient Egypt and its connection to our current planetary evolution. Soon after that, I received a profound visit from high-level beings who used ancient mystical technology to make a change in my life. I am alluding to the tools from the old times, often called rods and staffs.

Interdimensional practice session

The first incident was quite unexpected and tied to the other events that were coming right on its heels. It was a dimensional encounter with three people that was left deeply etched in my memory. It was not a dream but an event with a consciousness different than those found in waking and sleep states. Significant messages can be passed through this state of awareness, and these encounters often are a prelude for events that come to pass in our lives. They are like practice sessions for something that is scheduled to occur.

In this situation, I recognized one of the people as a highly regarded speaker I had never met but had seen in a video that talked about possible Earth changes. I'll call him Scott. He was accompanied by a woman with short, shoulder-length blondish hair. There were four of us altogether, but I cannot recall anything about the fourth person except that it was a man. We were traveling, trying to take someone to a sacred place. There was something about a book of divine origin, but I can't recall the details.

I was responsible for handling the travel to this mysterious destination. When Scott appeared, I notified him that I had made arrangements for four. He emphatically told me to go get the remainder of the people; this was a sacred site that required twelve people to be present. (I remember thinking, "Why didn't you just tell me that in the first place?")

We arrived at a place that appeared to be in the desert. The ground was dusty, and we stood outside a large dwelling with no windows that seemed to be made of stone. Outside, people were bustling around, oblivious to us. Suddenly, I don't know how, but we were inside the building. We spent time traveling down corridors looking for the "right path." Whatever we were looking for, we did not find it. This surreal setting seemed like a practice session for something, perhaps a rehearsal to prepare us for something to come in the future.

Oddly, a strange situation took place between Scott and me before the incident finished. He squeezed my arm and said, "You haven't gotten your body ready yet." I reminded him that I was working on it; I had been going to the gym regularly to build stamina and strength. Then he tried to show me what could happen if I achieved a desirable state of development involving my physique.

The essence of his eyes disappeared, leaving empty white corneas that shone brightly. It was as though his spirit had left his body. He started to encompass me in an embrace from behind, not a sexual embrace but a hug between friends. I tried to call him back (to his body) three times, but could only do it twice.

I awoke, recognizing the implication of being unable to evoke the third call. I wasn't ready for whatever it was we were being prepared to do; it would require a strong and healthy physique to successfully brave the trials that will be faced.

Recognizing the chambers

Weeks after this incident, I saw a flyer describing one of Scott's seminars and was given strong spiritual messages to attend. I relented and went, unsure of what would be accomplished. When he walked into the room with his wife, I choked. I had seen him in a video, which accounted for any rationalization I wished to assign to the event. But never before had I seen her. She was the same woman who was with him in the dimensional encounter. How else would I have known how she looked? It gave a creepy confirmation to all I had experienced.

Toward the end of the seminar, I began to figure out why I had been directed to attend. Part of the presentation was a slide show of Egyptian temples. One photo depicted an angular view of the Sphinx. I began to raise my hand to ask what would have been in the slide if he had extended the picture beyond its borders to a particular site. As I hesitated, not wanting to waste the participants' time with an inconsequential question, Scott proceeded to describe a hidden chamber at the same site I almost asked about. He then described a second chamber with greater enthusiasm, but the one I saw held greater consequence, although that may not be evident should these compartments be opened.

The otherworldly visitors had been teaching me to reach a particular harmonic sequence that they claimed, when initiated in the right spot with the presence of certain people, would grant entrance to chambers within the sacred sites of Egypt. It was not depth and control of vocal chords that held the key; rather it was directed by emotion radiated from the heart center, which in turn controlled the harmonics emitted by the voice—just like the ships that were driven by tones. I was unsure why they gave me this information and wondered if any of it was even true. Although I found the knowledge intriguing, I did not take it seriously.

He's baaack...

A particular slide got my attention. It showed two beings described as "immortals," as identified by a particular hieroglyphic marking on their bodies. The entity on the left was very familiar; I remembered him well. He was not of this Earth but was one of the Others. He could perhaps be referred to as the "Master of Race Relations" and was responsible for overseeing the early evolution of genetic seeding on this planet in its initial stages. Embracing his own ego, he became a DNA archetype, interbreeding with his choice of Earth's females. He came to Earth periodically, sometimes staying for extended periods. We would die and continue on in different lives and still he would be there, in full continuity. He invoked fear in many of the people. In retrospect, when beings do not have full understanding of each others' ways and one holds power over another, apprehension is an understandable reaction.

Seeing him opened up many memories of what went on in those early Egyptian years. Records may not be available to the public to reveal the genetic fiddling that occurred back then, but there is no mistaking the memories I have of those times. The claims of the others seem to be substantiated by my recall.

Rods and staffs

There were also pictures of items referred to as staffs and rods. I recognized those, too. They were used to scramble the vibratory essence of a person. Then the energy currents were rebuilt to redirect their spiritual or physical health. These tools could reduce a human being to no more than a primordial essence, seen in the ethers as just a symbolic code. I knew full well the critical element required to enact the power of this equipment was the skilled and disciplined use of the mind. It was a marriage of consciousness and technology. The tools could not be unleashed without the connection of a qualified intelligence.

It was not as much the using of the staffs that I recalled because I was trained in their employment. Rather it was that fateful memory of being struck at the apex of the neck with one. It was a sound and sensation that is carried within the eternal memory, never to be forgotten.

Ancient initiation tests

Scott also showed a picture of a secluded tunnel, now blocked off, that is hailed as the famed chamber where ancient initiation rites were administered. I remembered the secrets of this sacred site; it was a place that required knowing one's inner and true self. Critical preparation had to be completed before initiates were granted entry to this gateway to the cosmos. We had to be prepared to handle the vibrations we would face in there. We were readied for this by periods of fasting, accompanied by intense mental concentration. No solid food was ingested prior to the big event; students received only special concoctions of fluids with herbs in carefully prepared dilutions. Even these fluids were abandoned in the final preparatory stages.

The first encounter once the tests started was to meet your greatest fears. Whatever was held with the most horror and dread was brought forth to be faced in full reality. You were not allowed to proceed to further tests of mastery without passing this critical step because a soul could be needlessly lost forever if one did not master this trial. Many initiates only made it to this first phase; thus they wrongly carried memories into other lives that these tests were based on solely controlling fear. But there is much, much more beyond the conquering of one's most dreaded secrets.

What most people don't know is that once in that chamber, a portion of one's essence *never* leaves. You see, during the ceremony, a part of us becomes connected to a timeless vault in the universe that is, in some ways, beyond anything we can ever fathom. This crypt is a permanent anchor that can be re-accessed if you retain your mystical knowledge and powers between lives. An initiate can reclaim this time in other lives and return to this source.

If we successfully master the initial trials, and reach a particular stage in the testing, we can change our past, present and future lives. We access and recreate our entire evolution, including our existences in different time periods beyond the human experience. It is one of the supreme tests: We deliberately create and participate in parallel lifetimes.

If we become awake and self-aware during any of our lifetimes, we can return to this state of consciousness and access the links we established during our initiation trials. Essentially, we can "change the play" of our life by reprogramming our outcomes. This capability remains a master "get out of jail free" card available only to the most experienced time travelers.

This is why these high ceremonies remained so divine and hidden throughout time. In some ways, it was manifesting pure God presence because we divested authority into ourselves to create "life," with results ranging from primordial consciousness to a high state of evolution. However, we had to reach an advanced degree of personal evolution to be granted this initiation experience. It is one of the ultimate tests that many have never experienced.

Seeing those slides of Egyptian sites and relics triggered a response in me that brought forth many memories. The information had been tucked away, waiting for the right catalyst to bring it forth. Before I could mull over the implications of my remembrance, the next incident was about to unfold.

The family of Aton

I was washing up in the morning when suddenly I was told to stop. I began following motions that were sent to me and stretched my body in the suggested directions. These seemingly innocuous movements actually build an electromagnetic field unseen to the untrained eye. This field enables information to be transmitted by other beings as it is used like an antennae to send messages.

I followed internal guidance to light a candle on a table that had a picture behind it. I watched in amazement as my hands began to dance up and down in gentle swaying motions. The picture behind the candle was of a large orange sun with small rays around the outer rim. What I saw in the reflection of the picture was the sun manifest as my head. As my forelimbs went up and down, it appeared as if many arms were coming from the sun. They swayed gently and formed the Egyptian pose so often seen in hieroglyphics. The image looked like a God who would have been worshipped by primitive people. The sun was the head, with hands rotating around it as it rested on a female human body. I was then directed to pick up a dictation recorder and began to speak:

> *The spirit family of Aton has begun to gather to do the work of the time that is now arriving on the planet Earth. You are one of those children who has volunteered to go back to the Earth in a human form to help guide it through travails. For though you know and we know that these are but journeys and experiences, the human tends to look upon these situations as moments of difficulty because they require, in one sense, more work on the part of the entity who is going through the experience.*
>
> *The family of Aton has begun to gather. When we use the word Aton, it is but one concept; there are many. It is to help you understand certain characteristics and types of work that will be shared by groups of beings. So when we say family, you think in terms of the Earth concept but that is not the meaning. It is like an organization pattern to help you understand*[21] *those who will have tasks of the same nature, though not necessarily the same. For each of you has been trained, charged and worked with to fulfill certain aspects of the teachings about energy.*
>
> *The ties*[22] *will be similar to the way you know the concept of family. You have been shown this morning certain manifestations to understand concepts of communication within the time your coordinates reside. You have been shown that it is based on a manner of communicating that has been used throughout all of the false concepts of time. The sun was the symbol shown, used, and given to you. And you will understand the relationship of Aton. This concept was chosen because it is one within which your coordinates of reality are most familiar and enmeshed.*

Gaining greater understanding of what happened

Later that morning, I looked up Aton in the dictionary. I recalled that it was Egyptian and that it was a king or sun god, or the king who worshipped

---

21 Or recognize.

22 To each other.

the sun god. I was shocked to find that the book's reference to Aton described it just as they had shown me: human hands coming from a sun. The dictionary said:

"*Aton: A solar deity declared by Amenhotep IV to be the only god, represented as a solar disk with rays ending in human hands.*" It took me aback that the incident perfectly mirrored the definition of how Aton was depicted in those days.

This channeled information is difficult to understand due to their choice of words and the awkward sentence structure. Thus it requires explanation. The reference to where "your coordinates reside" addresses a concept called coordinates of reality. They are referring to how we are energy manifestations and our lives are established in points in time and space. To find someone in the cosmos, you can use the coordinates of reality like latitude and longitude readings. When they used the reference here, they were referring to how I now express myself as a life form.

The "false boundaries of space and time" refer to the knowledge that time and space are but concepts created by man to provide a sense of order and semblance to his existence.

The discussion about family concerns a term used to identify spiritual workers who have similar causes and tasks to accomplish. I knew of the historically recorded efforts of Akhnaten (also known as Amenhotep IV) to unify Egypt from a pantheon of collective deities to a singular God. But this message was chosen because I had soul-level knowledge of what truly happened at that time in history, and the cosmic reasons behind it.

That time was part of an extended drama designed to unfold over thousands of years to help the human species take an evolutionary leap. Electromagnetic changes were made about the planet then in preparation for energy grids that were to be firmly anchored approximately fourteen hundred years later when Christ would incarnate. Even then, it would still be only a prelude to another stage that would culminate in yet another two thousand years. At that time, the planet was scheduled to change its position in a dimensional field and man would be catapulted to a new evolutionary stage of awareness. We are being readied for this third stage in this lifetime; many of us incarnated during the other two times and assisted in those historical years. This was what they meant by the comment "a grouping to help you understand certain characteristics and types of work that will be shared by groups of beings." It was about the many groups of people, all busily working with their own tasks, who know they are all linked to help to accomplish the same mission. Although it's difficult to understand their words, the above source knew I would understand the message.

Are Earth changes to come?

The reference to the work of the time made me uneasy. Earlier in my life, I had been told spiritually there would be times of great change on Earth while I lived and this is what they were alluding to. I also read of this portent in many books by different authors. It was preferable to think of the possibility of a radically changed life as only a fantasy. Yet I queasily likened it to the denial that must have occurred in pre-World War II Europe: "I am safe in my home. My family and job are my reality. Hitler will not affect me...." Watch as the home and lifestyle are replaced by hunger, pain, horror and cruelty. What once held life became a crucible of suffering and death. Every society maintains its wish for perpetuity and plenitude. Were we any different? Was this our threshold of change? They keep assuring me we can control our fate and influence our destiny, but will we?

Our religious history

Related to all this, they have taught me that our legacy about the roles of Jesus, the apostles and others are not quite what history shares. There seems to be different versions, with slightly different twists, held in parallel universes. I have explored the role of the disciples and other followers and saw that they helped to prepare their society for stronger electro-magnetic energy patterns that were about to encircle the earth. These patterns would not culminate their full strength until approximately two thousand years later. These currents were from magnetic fields in space that washed over the earth the way waves pass through the ocean. Somehow, during the time of Jesus, they were able to be anchored around the earth with some type of attractive force holding them in place.

I was surprised to learn that many of the people close to Jesus were not simple peasants following an enlightened being, but spirits who held much mystical knowledge. Many of them previously lived at the time of

Akhnaten, almost fourteen hundred years prior and remembered they had started a process for the evolution of this planet that would happen in three phases. The reign of Akhnaten was the first phase and the time of Christ was phase two. They knew they were part of a team effort to prepare man for an eventual evolution of consciousness that would involve changes even in the physical manifestation of his body. They knew exactly what they were doing and used their awareness to create events that were recorded as miraculous. The one we know as Jesus was called Yeshua, and he relied on this team to augment his own mystical abilities. The most advanced members were not the known disciples, but quiet people whose names and eminence have long since disappeared into the silent records of posterity.

There is a lot of information about the time of Christ that does not match the allegory recorded in the bible and religious books. The Others say that the truth of that period is hidden away but has been hinted at through time. They have recently, over the past few decades, subtly influenced the media and literature to gently offer alternatives to what we now believe. Controversially, they suggest that the true records are already in the hands of the Vatican. Soon, they say, more historic accounts will be revealed that will further cloud the issue for some, while clarifying it for others. The truth will be clearly evident for those who wish to see it, while those who will not want to give up their staid beliefs will tenaciously fight to retain the old stories.

I have not been shown too much about whatever the truth may be, except that the "cast of characters" is, according to them, not what it seems. The roles of both the Mary's, James, Joseph and others have been obscured and are purported to be quite different from the truth. It seems that the whispered legends of Jesus having had children and leaving behind a royal bloodline on this Earth is true. What will be even more disconcerting to some is that alien life was significantly involved in the events that passed. As I have said repeatedly throughout this book, I am not proposing that this information must be accepted, but I am just sharing knowledge I have been exposed to in my journeys with other beings. I know that this topic is highly controversial and in no way intend to dogmatically assert something as truth, especially when I do not know what the truth is.

A visit from the High Order

The next part of these connected sequences unfolded rather quickly. The familiar feeling that happens during a visit began in the midst of sleep one night. I regained consciousness as I was summoned back to full awareness. The noise that plays silently within began to grow, along with the accompanying sensation when dimensions are altered for communication.

I remember being struck by one of the ancient Egyptian rods at the apex of the neck during another lifetime, but felt it as if it was now. I recognized the concentric waves of energy that rang around me, the deafening sound heard within the silence of my head, the blankness as I was returned to nothing but primordial energy then reprogrammed at every level. I remembered all this and more as my body felt everything in a moment of shared consciousness.

Suddenly, I was outside my body and everything appeared all right, although I had an uneasy feeling. Walking into the bedroom, I bent down toward the energy figures of my cats, comforted by their presence. Stroking them, they became odd clumps of energy and dispersed. Other energy forms appeared, and I strove to focus on the light.

Suddenly this state of being dissipated as I was brought back to my body in full consciousness. They snapped the wall to let me know it was them, just as they had done when we began.

I had just received a visit from the High Order. I do not fully understand what this "High Order" is, but I do recognize its significance in regard to exceptional universal power. Memories of the rods released at that seminar had initiated the event like a latent, hidden time-clock within my consciousness. My recall of Egypt, triggered by the seminar slides, was activating me in some way.

The next day, I looked at a black and white picture that had recently come into my possession. It had been discovered in a scrapbook after my father died. The snapshot was me at perhaps five years of age, resting in my first childhood bed, the site where "they" came to get me each night. But there was something odd about the picture. It had a strange energy field, far more active than other photographs, with a life of its own, as though you could actively step inside the scene. The emanation was so vibrant that I insisted on taking the picture out of the scrapbook despite the objections of family members.

After this "visit," the energy field around that picture was less intense and lay flat. The image appeared grayer, the prickling force surrounding the photo was no longer evident. It was then that the Others channeled something incredible. They explained that the force field was far too strong, that the picture had to be altered for protection. Left untouched, an energy source could penetrate into that dimension and alter events, meaning the path of my life, which in turn would effect who I had become today. It was preventing the past from interfering with the present, much like in the movie *Back to the Future*. During the visit, whoever was present had rods in hand, and they had been used to realign the picture.

Getting ready for the big visit

In a short time, I relived forgotten initiation protocols, trampled through what seemed to be an ancient hallway in a sacred temple, and experienced the rods, a hybrid technology of consciousness and machinery from age-old civilizations. I was being prepared, something was about to happen, but I hadn't a clue what it was. Unbeknownst to me, they were about to tell me. I was going to directly learn of their plans because they were about to visit and make their intentions known. They were going to tell me they are getting ready to let the world know they are here.

Chapter Twelve

Contact Unveiled

The date was March 13, 1997, and hundreds of people reported seeing strange lights in the sky over Phoenix, Arizona. Some say the lights followed them while they were driving; others just watched as they hovered over the city and blinked on and off. Home-video buffs recorded the event, trying to obtain evidence of whatever it was. Several of the pictures revealed something that some say was three miles long and V-shaped. More than one national newspaper carried the story but not until many weeks later. The controversy over what it might have been stirred up quite a few people, yet there never was a satisfactory, official explanation.

Ironically, the night it occurred I was coming back from a UFO lecture held in Sedona. I had never been to a UFO lecture before, but my friend convinced me it would be fun to go. I never saw the lights, even though they were sighted right near my house. I didn't even know anything had happened until a full week afterward. That was when something made me inquire if anything peculiar had occurred locally. I almost wish I had never found out about the Phoenix lights because then maybe I could deny what happened to me that next week.

On March 19, I went to bed about 11 p.m. It seemed to be a benign, quiet night—or so I thought. I settled into a comfortable sleep, unaware that anything was about to happen. Around 1 a.m., I felt myself being dragged from a dream into full consciousness. I immediately knew what was happening; I recognized the sound and sensation of a visit. After all these years, I still have not fully adjusted to the occurrence. It happens more gracefully, and I have greater control than when I was younger, but my psyche still experiences a modest amount of surprise and disbelief.

As I was waking, I knew I was having visitors, but I had no idea what was about to transpire. In all my years, in all of my experiences, this was the most startling and dramatic thing I ever had happen.

There were many of them in my room. Some were by the bed on both sides, others were out on my balcony. One seemed to be coming through the wall as I came to. I have always wanted to forget when I have a visit but that year they decreed I was to remember. They had recently started to wake me instead of taking me out from a sleeping state, so I could not deny them as readily. We had always worked cooperatively, and it was generally a loving environment. Not this time. There was an ambiance of severity that pervaded the air.

The training rehearsal

I recall being present at a meeting with hundreds of other humans. In retrospect, this bothers me. Where are the others? Who are they? Why don't they remember and come forward? I have no idea where I was, but we were all lined up in several rows, almost in formation. We were told we were being tested to see how well we could recall specific training we had been given over our lifetimes to work their technology. Each of us had a partner and we were assigned to activate small three-seater space craft. My associate was a young African-American male who may have been only 14 years old. I recognized him from prior dreams; we were always on what seemed to be an airship. Now I suspect they were not dreams.

Recall

I don't know what the other people there were told, but I do recall what happened to me. They had a lot of information, and it was given in pieces.

First, I was informed that I would no longer be allowed to dismiss and repress my work with others not of this planet. They said the time had come, and I must have complete recall. They then showed me a life review.

They revealed all the visits and interactions I had this lifetime. As they were about to start this, I recall arguing heatedly with them. In fact, I remember saying, "No f—ing way. I am not going through this."

In retrospect I find it kind of funny, in a juvenile type of way, that I swore at them. I received back the telepathic response, "Way." In other words, I had no choice and this was going to happen. Generally my wishes were respected in things of this matter, but not now. They said it was "time," and I was being brought into "full activation," in accordance with schedule, whatever that means.

They showed an extensive review of all my training since I came to Earth. Oddly, as I watched the scenes play out in my mind, they were familiar. I was not a stranger watching an odd exhibit but a person remembering, filling in holes that had previously been covered up. I saw my teachings of consciousness, science, space, time, inner nature, other dimensional cultures and much more. I was grateful and humble to have received such an extensive education. I also saw my participation in biological and genetic experiments. My higher self was concerned with the evolution of all species, not just the earth's human version. I have never been harmed and have no regrets over these events. I learned from the results just as they did. I have a scientific mind that is always inquiring; through these events I was able to increase my knowledge of cellular metabolism and regeneration, reproductive processes beyond human gestation, and vibratory alignment techniques to heal a physical body. The implications for health and medicine are extraordinary.

Prophesy

After this review, I somehow wonder if my teachers changed. The training event and subsequent recall episodes were rigid and devoid of play. The tone of the visit now became much kinder. This next set of information was gentler, less austere, but no less significant. I was given very specific information that I was directed to embed in my mind and recall when I returned.

They explained the acceleration of a recent rash of UFO sightings. They said they were preparing humans to accept that they, meaning other intelligent life forms, were definitely here. Although many people already were believers, had direct experiences or were just open minded, many more were not. A significant portion of our population are still very scared or believe that they are the only thinking, self-aware life in the universe. These visitors stressed they believed it was important that awareness of other intelligent life be done in a non-threatening way. Therefore, a strategy was chosen to gradually increase the number of sightings and encounters over time.

They showed me that the next phase was planned as a coordinated event, with several non-human species participating. I saw a scene during the day, perhaps late afternoon, that showed airships filling the sky across key points over the world. It was a simultaneous display held to irrefutably demonstrate their presence in our solar system. They said that my visit that evening and others like it (such as the Phoenix lights) were in preparation for this coming event; they were slowly accelerating evidence of their involvement with our planet. They emphasized this plan was tentative and might change, dependent on how events on Earth come to pass. They do not want to come forward until they are "invited." By this they mean acceptance on a mass scale needs to occur before they will come forth as planned.

They also said at the time they were meeting with me, they had representatives meeting with key leaders throughout the world. I was told that President Clinton and Boris Yeltsin were in Helsinki, Finland, being briefed about what would eventually happen.

After discussing the preparation for global contact, they explained something they said would have significant impact on our planet. They knew I was aware that future events were no more than probabilities and that nothing was concretely established. Maybe that is why they showed me this information—they knew I would not take it out of context and would regard it with the appropriate level of concern. Not fanatically but with scientific detachment.

They proceeded to tell me about a "triune setting," which was something that was about to occur. It was a triangular shaped portal that was somehow affiliated with three events on earth. The first corner of the setting represented the portal itself; it was aligned with this opening that they said happened ever so rarely, once every few hundred years at best.

The second tip of the portal was anchored to a serious event they said might happen. This is a calamitous event on earth, one with enough severity to change life on the face of the planet for every human. While they conveyed this information, I saw pictures of what I thought was the Middle East and somehow felt they were referencing a nuclear event that would trigger an even more serious event on the planet. I couldn't help but wonder if the continuously escalating hostilities over there resulted in a nuclear event, would cataclysmic earth changes be provoked? What if there was a tenuous fault line on a major tectonic plate in that vicinity? During the earlier training affair, they expressed they were very concerned about a potential for some event to trigger an ice age that would descend over the planet within forty-eight hours. The temperature would drop so quickly and significantly that much of life would be wiped out. They were concerned about the survival of our species. Could their concern about rapidly plummeting temperatures have been related to this possible occurrence?

The third setting of the portal was tied to what they said was the impending discovery of previously hidden documents that would reveal our true history and destiny. They said it would change our lives forever. I was telepathed a picture of the Sphinx and pyramids in Egypt, so I suspected it may be related to the opening of reputed hidden chambers said to exist in those dwellings. There have been many claims of catacombs connecting concealed chambers that some believe hold documents of unknown times. I have had other visits and transmission of knowledge related to this, but as usual, I always remained a bit doubtful no matter what outrageous paranormal activity I experienced.

I was returned to my bedroom about 3-3:30 a.m. I was frightened as well as angry and just stayed there for the next two hours, staring vacantly into space, convincing myself the event never occurred. Finally, about 5:30 a.m., I picked up the tape recorder and began to record what happened. But by then I had lost many of the rich details.

Reflection

I continued to mull over the implications of what they said about their contact with the two world leaders. I found this shocking and odd. Why would they impart this information to me? If it was true, were they working with them in full consciousness?

In retrospect, I have many questions and doubts. Did I make it up? No, I know something happened. However, I am unsure what actually did occur. I could have had a "holographic insert" implanted to make me think that the event took place. This is like watching a movie then being convinced you lived the story. However, I was unnerved to discover the next day that President Clinton really was meeting with Boris Yeltsin in Helsinki at that time. I felt like throwing up when I learned that information. Was I told that just to prove the visit really happened? Could I have seen the information somewhere and then my mind was scanned, and the contents fed back to me as if it was new information? I believe I had heard that a summit meeting was scheduled but did not know it was occurring then.

Looking back, the whole thing sounds preposterous and paranoid. I think there is no way that anything happened. Unfortunately, I know that it did.

What are the implications of this event? Well, if it is true, then we might be facing some very interesting times ahead of us. If it's not, who or what was able to accomplish this influence over me?

Previously, I told only selected people about what happened, cautious that it sounded farfetched and could label me as a UFO crazy. I hesitated to speak about it for fear of accusations that I made up the alleged event to self-aggrandize myself. However, if I am that creative, then I amaze myself.

I have had several opportunities to come forward, including an open mike session at a meeting held in Phoenix by one of the more well-known personalities on the UFO circuit. I deliberately chose not to speak of my experience in that situation. The crowd seemed based in emotionalism rather than scientific inquiry. I also spoke with a couple of men who say they are UFO researchers but found them to be no more than casual interviewers, making a living off the UFO phenomenon. I was dismayed they did not seem to use academic scientific research methodology. The UFO crowd is filled with many intelligent, inquiring people but also has its allowance of representatives intent on proving their own agenda. I do not wish to unwittingly become a part of anybody's personal campaign. I will not proselytize to the world that this message is the "truth" and that people must respond to it. Instead, I choose to prudently share what happened and offer it for consideration. I have a strong aversion to purveyors of "doomsday" information and do not intend to become one. Besides, they have taught me how to control conscious awareness to "program" the reality that we bring unto ourselves. This control over fate is something they want all humans to realize.

I am choosing to share what I have experienced in the hope that others will not have fear. If I can help people understand multidimensional experiences, then I am honored to be of service in that arena.

Chapter Thirteen

Implications For Mankind

Where does all this leave me? I know that my work with these other races is not finished but only just beginning. Whoever, whatever these beings are, they have been teaching me about the science and mysteries of the universe. I have been instructed in inter-dimensional travel, wormhole navigation, parallel universes, translating universal coding patterns, technology powered by harmonics, genetic manipulation, intergalactic cultural variation and the power of consciousness to create self-awareness. Truly, it has been a full curriculum.

If what I have been shown by these other beings is accurate, then our history began many eons ago on this planet, when seeding of the human race occurred. Twelve extraterrestrial life species contributed DNA strands to create our bodies. We started out as a genetically tinkered race designed to be workers. Initially sterile, incapable of reproduction, we were eventually allowed to reproduce. Over time, with their oversight, we underwent evolutionary processes; on numerous occasions they manipulated pairings between genetically desirable men and women to advance the human species. In some ways they regard us as their children and claim creative rights, but they also recognize our ultimate sovereignty.

We reached a pivotal point twice during the past few thousand years, once during the time of Akhenaton and again during the life of Jesus.

During these periods, the consciousness of a group of self-aware spirits embodied and anchored electromagnetic fields that were activated around this celestial orb. These fields have the capability to interact with our cellular genetics. Pulsing radiation from sources within our galaxy has acted as a trigger to help set off a cosmic time clock, working with the electromagnetic waves anchored to the planet. This has released genetic mutations in our cells that have accelerated human capabilities.

As I consider what has been shown to me, I find it interesting and possible. My teachings about parallel universes and the changing nature of time has shown me that there is no one precise answer for our true origins. Perhaps my recognition of this was another one of their tests.

I think we are beings in the midst of an evolutionary cycle, who are just beginning to discover our true roots. Along with these roots comes some jarring discoveries, similar to a child discovering that mom and dad aren't his or her real parents. The Spiritual Elders say:

You are evolutionary adolescents and this is your puberty.

They are here among us

We have entered into a time when a new awareness has begun to unveil itself. A change in mass consciousness seems to be slowly spreading as we contend with global evolution. At this time, it appears there are many voices that will talk to whoever will listen. It's as if a cosmic FCC just opened up a large number of new bandwidths, but the communications are on a different frequency and you don't need a radio or TV to receive the transmission. As a species we are now in a stage of evolution that allows us to be receptive to information available through this method of transmission.

Discretion and respect

It's imperative to note that if we hear a voice from another realm, it is still our responsibility to carefully exercise two of the most valuable gifts of the human condition: discernment and discretion. We must use our judgment to determine what is best for our reality and the beliefs we establish for our lives.

Therefore, I request that each of you look deep within your soul to determine what is truth at this time. We can respect each other's version without necessarily embracing it as our own. Information may come from sources external to customary resources, but just because they are not living humans does not mean the resource must necessarily carry greater wisdom than our own. (It has been my experience that it often does, however.) Discernment and discretion are vital aspects of the human experience.

The test is to recognize our own power as a species without deifying external messengers who may have advanced knowledge or technology. It will be easy to relinquish responsibility to go within to find truth when multiple external resources may be about to flood consciousness with different ways of understanding life as we know it.

We no longer have to choose between Kansas and Oz to find our answers. Like the Tin Man, the Lion and the Scarecrow, we must find our Dorothy to help us realize the secret is that love is everywhere, fear is an illusion, and brains are relative. We must learn, however, that Dorothy will not be an alien, a book or a prophet, but that she lives inside each of us. The only tools necessary on this next trek of our collective journey are consistent self-awareness and a good, pure heart.

With these words, I close this journey.

Part Two:

The Teachings Of The Spiritual Elders

Introduction

In the second half of 1996, after a lengthy absence, I began to channel once again. The content was different than before and encompassed longer treatise about specific topics. Many of the messages focused on social issues. I have included abbreviated explanations about each dialogue to help readers better understand the communication. May you enjoy the words of other worlds as they are shared for our benefit.

THE NATURE OF CHANNELING

This discourse holds the most reasonable explanation I ever encountered about what happens when one channels messages. Hopefully, the content will be helpful to those who have not experienced this phenomenon.

When the information comes through, it can be compared to entering a connective formation. I ascend into an altered state, and my consciousness rises up as I become increasingly relaxed and enter into a deep meditative state. At a unique point, there is a connection, a silent "click," described only as a sound without sound. At this juncture we become a hybrid of a collective essence. There is no "me" or "them." Just "we," just "us," just all that is.

It's misleading when others refer to being "only a channel" and take no responsibility for the information that comes through. It's a little like the ventriloquist blaming the dummy. As the following message shows, the person is a filter through which all information borrows his or her color of bias and knowledge. This needs to be acknowledged.

I will not identify a name or source for these messages that come through, because labels tend to cloud one's mind and develop predetermined associations. It is the message, not the messenger that carries import here. Profound speech can come from a young child, an old fool, or an ordinary citizen with no outstanding public acclaim. It doesn't matter.

As a society, we tend to deify our messengers, and I refuse to let that happen. It is of no consequence whether the source is George of New Jersey, Avedon of Aventura, Ascended Masters, or Intergalactic Warriors. I ask only that you listen to the harmonies; if the song is sweet to your ears, hold it within your heart. If it carries no import, discard it.

It must be remembered that an entity can only teach that which is within its realm of experience. To rely on another for areas beyond its reach of knowledge, that expand beyond the scope of the entity's awareness, will result in limitations in the accuracy of the transcribed information.

If I were to relay to you that traffic was clear as I sat in my small Honda[23] *waiting to take a left-hand turn, yet the view was obscured by a tall semi-truck, I would not know that a sports car was zipping up the side at a rapid speed. If I proceeded, based on that navigational warning, without any assessment of my own, I could perhaps be in a very serious accident, one that could cost my mortality.*

We have much the same responsibility here on Earth to use our own guidance tools and senses, to be aware of what life's journeys might bring. For the speeding car can come at any time and if we abrogate our responsibility to look for ourselves, we could end up in a state with very serious repercussions.

A channeled entity is not the ultimate resource for knowledge. There is absolute truth, universal truth and personal truth. The channeling source can only share what is known from its sources and experiences gained from its travels. While it may provide good information in some areas, please regard it as only an adjunct resource, and not an end-all, be-all omnipotent fount of knowledge.

There are many probabilities and tendencies, each one impacting the past, present, and future simultaneously. What may be desire in one realm can be actuality in another. There is nothing other than infinite

---

23 I found it fascinating that they said "small Honda" rather than "a small car." For 10 years I drove a white Honda Accord. At the time of this message I drove a different car, which I'd had for just a few years. Obviously, the Accord was more deeply ingrained in my consciousness because that was the memory accessed.

possibility, a concept that many otherworldly and earthly resources forget to include in their discourses about self-proclaimed truths.

In channeling information, it also comes through the viewer of the otherworldly entity and the translator, so it is given only after passing through two filters. Again, a word of caution.

In this situation, we become a hybrid, an amalgamation where the knowledge, wisdom, and experience of the one still in earthly form is combined with our collective experience. Because this is one who has devoted her life to the higher learning[24] *and has her own version of collective wisdom, an ideal triad is made between the father, the son, and the holy ghost, to borrow one of your sayings.*

Generally, as information is passed through the organ that functions as her brain, in a momentary instant she regards it as if it were her own thought and is able to synthesize it through her filter, thus adding a perception that may help it to be understood better by earthlings. So we see this as beneficial and an enhancement rather than as interference, for we are ever ready to supersede should it be necessary. For instance, she did not understand the above reference to the father, son, and holy ghost but did not interfere and edit it out from the text. We do the same for her additions and deletions, sending soft messages that are sensed in regard to whether the essence of a message has been changed from the effort to edit a sentence to enhance understanding.

For at this time, our exploration of the resources found within the mind is sometimes not smooth in your terms, a sentence may be incorrectly established in the attempt to synthesize vocabulary to complete a thought transmission.

---

24 Refers to me as the channeler.

We use the hybrid approach for many reasons, resonance being one. But it is also a time on your plane when it can be seen that this effort is one which may be attained by all men who seek. There is nothing special or mystical. Did not one say to you, "Everything I do you can do and more?"

So by using the scientific and other knowledge which she has graciously amassed during her lifetime, she can be an active participant in the process. Her renaissance learning, as well as the gleaning of projects of your times, is of great benefit to us as we use her as a willing channel to translate higher truths back to your plane.

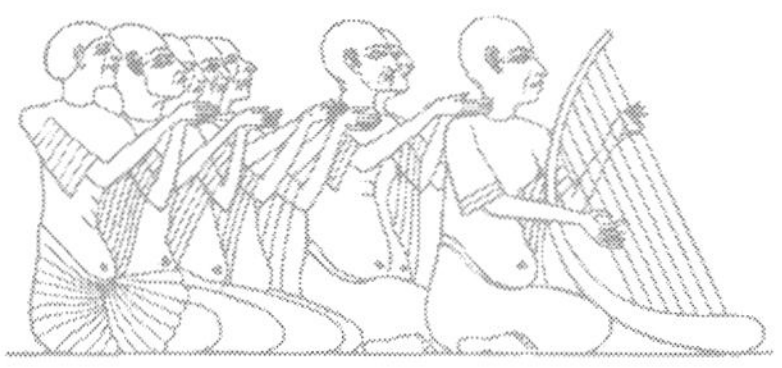

LOVE, MARRIAGE & EXTRICATION FROM RELATIONSHIPS

The following information came through for a friend who was having a lengthy love affair with a married man. I believe it is one of the most profound, provocative, and deepest truths of these teachings.

> *The true test is understanding the laws of God versus the laws of man. The ability to differentiate between the two marks a level of awareness to which many aspire but which most are not able to understand. Man tries to interpret the laws of God but in doing so often ends up with inaccurate explanations.*
>
> *Entities are placed here for the purpose of spiritual growth. Therefore, it is the responsibility of the spirit to continuously grow. To do so meets God's intent and thus God is honored. Difficulty is encountered when a situation is no longer productive and is not conducive to learning and growth, but man's institutions teach that the situation should be prolonged.*
>
> *Marriage is an example of this type of situation. "Till death do us part" is a component of the vows taken by many Americans. Interpretation of this phrase, compounded by religious teaching, results in a belief that to end a union is to break the promise not only to the partner but also to God.*
>
> *God did not intend to have a being wither away in a loveless, empty union between souls. This drains the entity when it should be filled with learning experiences.*

Rather, this situation is often encountered when a being must learn the test of strength. Strength is built in recognizing the lack of productivity—even harm—of perpetuating a situation where there is no more growth. Further strength occurs when action is taken. While man's institutions teach of the rightness of continuance of such a union, God's will, if followed, would be to end the relationship and find the courage to have faith in the next leg of the journey of life's adventure.

When God spoke of a union that was made in heaven and would be broken by no man, he was not referring to the unions on Earth that occur with frequency between men and women. There are spirits that are bound to each other, often by points of origin. It is to these unions that reference was made to the immortality of the conjoining. For no matter how they, or others, may try, there is no breaking the bonds of these bound souls (with the exception of ascension).

When an encounter of this nature occurs (bound souls), it is a most beautiful gift. For many search, but seldom find, this apex of the experience of earthly love. If the beings act forth with honor and the highest of intentions, the unity between the two is right and should occur. The beings should recognize the gift of mutual existence in the Earthly dimension at a concurrent time reference and be grateful at the opportunity to join in union. It is God's intent that the souls recognize and pursue the relationship.

It should be noted that the lesson often lies not in the blending of the two souls who lie in recognition of each other, but of the process employed to extricate oneself from situations that lie in obstacle of the union. The disengagement should be of the highest manner and done in an honorable fashion. If the test of honor is failed, then the union between the bound souls will not have the success that will be seen by those who pass the test.

When lying occurs, it indicates an unwillingness to face the consequences of one's actions. An evolved being understands the repercussions of lying. It is similar to cheating on an academic entrance exam. One may gain admittance to the academy, but there will be a lack of skills necessary to sustain one's self and to overcome future tests. Awareness entails acceptance of conditions and situations. It is the acceptance of the situation and the using of one's judgment that is of issue, not the manipulation of events to ensure a desirable outcome chosen by the entity.

Therefore, it is of importance, in extricating oneself from the decaying relationship that honesty is employed. This entails not only an absence of lying but also of recognition of being true to one's emotions. Attempting to couple with one partner when one's heart lies with another is an example of not being true to the situation and is unjust to all involved.

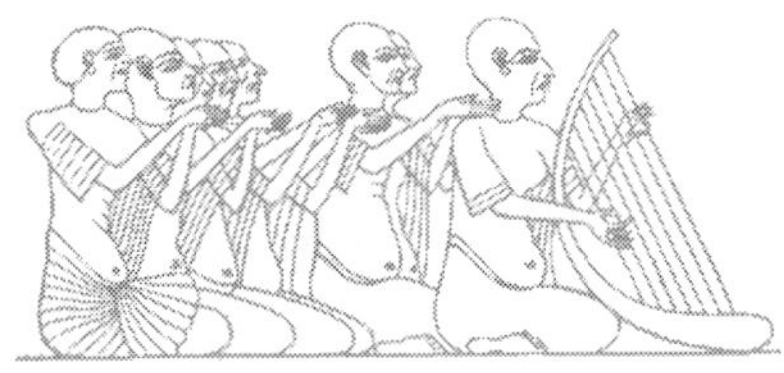

Epochal Relationships

This transmission came through during a time when the source continued to dwell on human relationships. It foretells of a re-emergence of strengthening ties between men and women and expresses the need for more than one primary partner in a life that will be filled with experiences characterized by distinct epochs of personal growth.

> *Relationships are epochal. Much has been written regarding the changes in the polarities between men and women on Earth at this time in your period of development. Mr. Zukav gave beneficial information when he spoke of units occurring for the time period of alignment between the souls.*[25] *For most people, this will encompass approximately three Earth mates, mostly of the opposite sex.*
>
> *By epochal we mean that they cover epochs, or periods of growth, in the lives of persons on Earth. While a significant relationship may occur, one that previously could have been evidenced by the ceremony of marriage, it is being recognized that the spurts of growth in the human condition may be benefited by different partners to help aid the development of each person.*
>
> *Therefore, rather than spend time working out dead end situations that have no growth where the lesson is one of extrication, one should separate in a comfortable*

25 They are referring to Gary Zukav's book, *The Seat of the Soul.*

manner to allow each partner to be free to pursue the next level, or epoch, in the growth of the soul that is manifesting as a human entity. The manner of co-joining financial resources will be handled in a new manner to accommodate this new phenomenon. Laws will be written in the future, and your culture will be ready to accept preparation of not only the joining of souls for growth but the just as important separation. Please refer back to our discourse on the extrication of a being from a loveless, empty union.

There will be those who will function as mates but in a non-sexual way. This will be for a period of learning that will occur as men and women reach out to each other to explore new depths. This means that many of the relationships that occur in the future will be established on the foundation of friendship. The soul does this to feel safe interacting with the innermost aspects that people often choose not to open up for fear of the depth of feeling that may be revealed.

This time of learning about each other in a manner that is not accustomed by your people is one portion of an evolutionary phase that is being accomplished en masse. As the transitional aspects occur, a speeding up of underdeveloped areas has happened. Men and women, polarity rotations of our own being, are being explored from a duality, yet also from a singularity. By that we mean that memories are being opened to remind selves of the duality of their own being. For are not men comprised of a partial feminine essence and vice versa? Rather than a separation of the heart, there is a union that is unrecognized. It is in recognizing this combined essence (mutually comprised essences of male and female components) that unions, partnerships will have greater success.

By allowing the opening of love to flow into the essence of men, into the body that one now inhabits, unique feelings and depth of being can occur. All lessons are being stepped up in preparation of the transformation. For as one gets ready to go to the carnival to ride the roller coaster, care is taken not to eat beforehand and to empty one's bowels. Metaphorically speaking, the same thing is occurring. A cleaning out of the spiritual toxins, a preparing to accomplish one's lessons, to be ready to go on to the next step is occurring. That is the reason behind the restlessness and the pressure and the self-induced illnesses occurring within many at this time. For if one is not "getting" the message, the physical body is being used to convey the symptomology that will reveal the key to the heart of the true issue in need of being resolved.

REPRESENTATION IN A ONE-WORLD GOVERNMENT

While sitting on my balcony during a moonlit night, I was overwhelmed with an urge to begin writing about a unified world government. I quickly got my laptop and let the information come through.

> *This is an article written before its time. The concept of one-world government.*
>
> *It cannot be afforded to have skewed political interests governing the world in the upcoming new order, for it shall be a precarious time, with the stake of global survival at risk. The world will need to learn to accept different priorities, values, and mores, many which will challenge the very souls of the inhabitants of the planet.*
>
> *In the new order of things, human representatives will be called on to assist in the governance in a multicultural way to which they are not accustomed. Rather than work to further their own sovereign cause, they will be required to collaborate to ensure continued survival upon the Earth. Because this new process will require a set of skills that have not been valued in recent history, a process should be established to facilitate representation that would be beneficial for governance of ALL stakeholders, rather than having a select few with narrow interests push their agenda to the forefront to the detriment of the entire body.*
>
> *Each culture values different aspects of human development and personality; hence, what a Muslim*

background may prefer could potentially be antithetical to an American. Even in the United States, there remains a spectrum of oppositional viewpoints regarding righteousness, spirituality, and leadership to the point of bloodshed and desire of eradication of one's enemies. Therefore, the propensity that the development of the world order will be guided by external resources is a situation that has been brought on by refusal to evolve as a whole to a certain level.[26] *There will need to be an element of shock to promote cohesiveness and action in a unified manner.*

This responsibility requires tenets of wisdom. Wisdom is not grown. It is not found in politically misguided souls, errant relatives, good old friends and people of only one color or gender. No, for this government shall hold the fate of not just man, but all species within its command.

How does one go about finding the representation that will have the correct balance of old age wisdom, common sense, charisma, astuteness, intelligence, and importantly, a sense of humor? By a process of checks and balances. A vote of the people is not adequate for the seriousness of this job as witnessed by the self-indulgent, misguided souls that have been voted for in all countries, especially the United States.

After self or external recommendation, candidates should undergo scrutiny of a search group comprised of qualified individuals who must embody many of the characteristics sought in the candidate. This group alone should be rotating in membership and undergo a similar procedure for participation in execution of its responsibilities to avoid political bias and manipulation of the process.

---

26 They are referring to oversight by off-planetary species that will help guide us into a new way of governance.

There should be criteria established that defines the candidate's qualities and all scoring evaluations should be open to the public. No aspects should occur in private. The selection of candidates should be honed to a chosen few, from whom the best qualified shall emerge.

Desirable Characteristics & Qualities

- *Proven ethics*
- *Community involvement*
- *Expert decision-making capability*
- *Sensitivity to all people of conditions and races, as well as other species*
- *Demonstrable understanding of human nature*
- *Capacity to act under crisis*
- *Environmental sensitivity and understanding*
- *Multilingual capability*

False Prophets And Egos

This discourse was directed at people who led parlor events to help others find spiritual "answers." I had encountered several who were ego-driven, wanting to be recognized as having the "true spiritual direction," rather than being a humble servant of God. One man began by saying that everyone was entitled to an opinion but if you were wrong, he would argue until you realized his truth.

> *Oh, Children of the White Light, oh, Father of the Sun. Let it be seen now that our time of work has begun. We are here to help the children of Earth begin in their endeavors to bring forth the time of changes upon this planet known as Earth. There are many of us now working together in a collective manner to activate the consciousness of those who are surrounding the circle of light upon this planet.*
>
> *Many of the circles have begun in small manifestations that have begun to spring forth from the homes of those who have been willing benefactors of the process. The messages are being imparted through many and are coming through with the most clarity from those who are least expected to be speaking. Those who take forth the light upon themselves and manifest as an ego presentation are still managing to complete the work of the Father but are distracting from themselves by being themselves.*[27]

---

27 Egotistical teachers with arrogant personalities detract from the spiritual message they try to convey.

These entities must learn and must remember to continue to work upon their fractal segments.[28] *They are no different from any others and perhaps their lessons are even stronger than those they profess to teach. Let them take heart from this message and listen to its eminence and remember that it is directed towards them. For all those who function in the ego, there is danger in letting an imbalance come forth. But this imbalance is a common manifestation upon the journey in which you have embarked. It is not unfamiliar to any of you, but again you must remember to use your inner harmonies to keep it in check; you will be able to do greater work when in complete balance. Those around who you profess to think of as your students are really your teachers. Let them reflect back to you that which you wish to profess to be. Allow them to be a mirror for you, so you may see the greatest lessons which you must overcome.*

For those of you who will hear this, it will hit upon the heartstrings. But for those who have deafened their ears, it will hit upon the heartstrings deepest of all. You shall hear this message and shall remember and know that this recall is aimed for you.

---

28 Fractal segments" refers to the personality or ego part of who we are. This component of ourselves is a part of a greater collective essence that comprises a larger consciousness of which we are just a component.

Illusions Of Wealth

Generally I can feel words rolling around inside of me before channeling, and my thoughts begin to dwell on the content. In this situation, I had no idea what this piece was going to discuss until we started it.

> *There is a time in every man's life when a choice must be made. This choice is in regard to following God or following the heart of the life path on Earth. This is a most difficult decision to be rendered, especially for the young spirits in heart. Choices always present a pathway that opens a new series of events to be taken into consideration. One must consider what is at stake during these opportunities that present themselves to a human soul: growth of the being versus growth of the inner fiber of one's aspect.*
>
> *These conflicts are, in reality, opportunities to continue to find God in the nearest and dearest way. A life without strife is truly the cruelest happening to the human soul, for opportunities are denied (that can bring about) growth. What some perceive as blissful happiness in the eyes of man is, in reality, a holding pattern that affords no growth to the individual. So you see, in reality, it is almost a cruel thing. The easy path is not so easy, for it holds one back from the true evolutionary pathway designed for your species.*
>
> *So judge not ever so harshly the spirits that have chosen a life of luxury. The illusion portrays a desirable happenstance, but the reality fills the heart with sorrow. The key is in not recognizing what are the true treasures*

on Earth. Hints, wisdom, and logic have all been available for eons of time, yet still the people of Earth choose to dwell in the illusion of a false mirror that reflects back no issues of work to be done.

Your illustrious presumption that the life of a Hollywood star or magnate is the one to be desired stares you in the face, but shallow empty shells are left as the legacy of these existences. In reality, they are the toughest journey of all, for it is man's desire to rise above a sumptuous lifestyle that shall prevail, and nothing else. In not recognizing these illusions remain falsehoods that do not endure with the passage of existence onto other paths of awareness.[29] *Your people continue to desire an empty tunnel within which they slide down to another level, rather than ascend up to the higher planes.*

29 *Upon leaving this life, the soul becomes aware that that the existence was superficial.

The Sacredness Of All Life

I had been encountering insects in my house. Trying to withhold my initial impulse to "step on them" or "squash them" was a most difficult task. It is much easier to wipe out bugs quickly, rather than capture and release them outdoors. Along with these encounters, I had a dream where I came upon a deadly scorpion. After dismembering it, I was heartbroken to watch it suffer as the life flow ebbed out. Even if it was only a dream, I was sorry I had killed it in such a ruthless manner.

You have chosen to undertake understanding of the sanctity of all life, a task which you at times find odious as you travel through the insect kingdom. In your taking of this life essence, you have been reminded of the sacredness of the life vibration which God emanates in all living things, even in objects with which your species has not yet learned to recognize consciousness of other kinds.

The Father has not created anything without loving thought that helped with the manifestation process. What may seem ugly or jarring to one species is in reality held with great beauty by another. A spider's web contains a delicate beauty of its own, wouldn't you say? Yet many of you hold the creator of the web, the magic spinner, with disdain, for its features frighten you. Yet in witnessing the web you are silently reminded that all creatures have their place and are beautiful in God's eyes, just as a mother sees nothing but special elegance in her own child.

So hold with respect, no matter how repugnant, how repulsed you may initially feel, the object in your sight. When beholding it, remember that it is another brother. For if you are all children of the same source, that results in bonds of brotherhood that your species has yet to fully understand in all its implications. Bless it, leave it, and be on your way.

The Evolution Of Man

Here the Others begin to reveal explicit details about their relationship to us. They begin to divulge information about DNA, cloning, evolutionary changes to the body, and karma. They claim to be the source of the noises (clicks and pops) around me that other people have also heard.

The complex information about karma merits a brief explanation. Traditionally, those who give credence to the concept of karma believe that relationships are established between people based on the contents of prior interactions in this life or in others. However, the Others say we can work out these connections with another person who is spiritually related. The connection is based on being part of the "family" unit, or spiritual grouping, also known as a monadal family.

While this is specifically directed toward me, I have included excerpts when information addresses generic concepts others could also learn from. As always, I caution you to please regard the information as only a possibility, rather than an absolute truth.

Genetic origins

> *This is a divine species*[30] *currently lost in its own transition of the events unfolding on this planet.*
>
> *We are ever-present in your domain due to the development of a frequency coding mechanism that enables us to chain back to you. You have allowed*

30 Humans.

yourself to see this only as DNA molecules, but it is far much more.

The intertwining helix has been developed to be unchained and redesigned to bring forth a higher evolved manifestation of yourself. Like a father looking at his son, you will soon face a new life in a body to which you are now unaccustomed. However, like wearing in a new suit or fit of clothes, it will become ever more comfortable for you to zip around in and it will suit the new vibration[31] *just fine. Do not fret; all is planned and will go according to divine will. This is the dawn of a new morning, truly as you say on your planet. Allow us to guide you in a manner that will be devoid of any pain or discomfort and you will find the transition most pleasant.*

We are your brothers, fathers, mothers and sisters, for we established the seed to bring you forth and brought you forth to this planet to colonize. Eventually you were left to reproduce and claim this planet as your own and as your home. In doing so we wiped the memory circuits clean and left you to your own devices, your own free will to find the evolution of your cosmic destiny. As you evolved to your current state within your current century, there was an illusion you were spawned upon this planet by natural evolutionary forces. That is not the case. We seeded you and designed you from a hybridization of multiple strands of what you would call DNA, only it is not DNA. That is the form of the replicator device in molecular components that is now within your body.

The seed was very different and composed of what we will reveal to you as 12 space races. You have been astute enough to detect we are withholding information

---

31 They are referring to the change in the frequency of Earth's vibration. It is supposed to shear into two planets, one of which will be a higher octave with a more harmonious civilization.

and that is correct.[32] *It is not time to let that piece come forth due to the evolutionary level on your planet this day.*

You are at a serious crossroads that is similar to the evolvement in the days of a time your legacy has termed Atlantis. The genetic manipulation is primitive but effective and you can now create life and combine it with technology. This is a serious step for any species, but you have yet to breed out the violent tendencies of your race, making this a dangerous point of evolution for you to be in. Like an adolescent whose body grew before the maturity was there, you now have "toys" that are dangerous. As you are about to leap forward to a new hive of dimensionalities,[33] *you are bringing with you undesirable attributes that must be cleansed before we can allow you to go to the next octave.*

We have established a collaborative effort among the "space brothers," as some of you like to call our collective entourage. We are working to watch and monitor your progress at this critical time.

The increased multiple (UFO) sightings around the world are designed to make you aware you are only one small piece of a much larger divinity. "Wake-up" we call to you for we cannot come near until you invite us and the invitation must come forth from within the heart center of your being. Thus, this process will continue and slowly accelerate, but no great showing can happen until you collectively reach a point of awareness and conscious control that invites us to share your domain. The inherent irony is we are actually with you the whole time, except you cannot perceive us as we can see you.

---

32 I sensed there was a lot of information they could share about this and telepathically asked to learn more about it. Instead, I received what felt like a powerful barrier in response to my request. Finally, they acknowledged they would not say anymore at this time because they do not want us to unravel this piece just yet. There is great concern about our cloning activities. Apparently we have uncovered certain techniques but they feel we have yet to gain the responsibility and understanding that should go with these scientific advances.

33 New understanding and experiences with different dimensions.

Karma

Many of your veils have been lifted to allow you to peer into the true cosmic collective essence of who you are. We have allowed you to see how energies are manifested collectively and singularly upon this Earth and translated into individual personalities. You have been shown how energy circuits can join unbeknownst to the personalities involved and collective work can be done.

This planet chooses to accept a collective concept it has termed "karma" for the workings of energy exchanges to maintain a neutrality and point of balance among different frequencies, energy streams, forms of consciousness, again what you call personalities among your people. Yet you have been shown how these can override individual circuits to become a singular collective essence, to use a conundrum. More plainly, a person can work out energy karma exchange with another person through the use of a third intermediary who is unaware of what is happening.

Reporting back on the human experience

We have trained you as you have excelled in your studies. Because of your rapid nature to detect and remember, we have been able to implant information that can be later translated back to your people on Earth.

As you decided to cooperate in a project, we have planted you—as well as many others—as an outpost collecting information transmitted back to our civilization on a regular basis, thus your continued conflict of, "Who am I? Why am I here? I don't seem to fit in anywhere." In many ways this curriculum has been easy for you, in an intellectual sense, but the emotional patterning has been especially difficult. You are not used to transmitting these patterns and they have scared you when you have felt the frequency modulation. At the same time, you have enjoyed the raw primitive feelings and experiences that we do not seem to have due to the difference of our existences and cultures, so to speak. This also has to do with the many numbers of frequencies we can reach that you cannot. It is a whole other experience, in the most literal and figurative sense.

Sound patterns stimulate states of consciousness

We are the ones signaling you with the knocks and clicks. This is a pattern of information that is more than it seems; it is a trigger to release certain chemicals into your bloodstream as your brain recognizes the sounds. Again the harmonics come into play. The sound frequency initiates a biological action that brings about a collective condition of memory and awareness to enable us to contact and communicate with you in a manner that is conducive to the suit you wear that is reliant on the five senses and the illusion of perception peculiar to your land.[34]

The ego fights change

You are about to go forth into a whole other realm of awareness. Be prepared for the changes it will bring. You have petitioned for this and your words have been heard. You have reached this level before in the Earth experience, and though you may feel fright at first, it will soon become very familiar to you and comfort levels will be established quickly. The fright is based from the ego who falsely believes it will die and lose control. Soon it integrates and sees it is not so bad as we go to the next level. But like an infant crying from a car seat that is soon lulled to sleep by the sound of the car engine, it will work to assist from its level to help you recognize essences that will be important to detect. So see, everything has

---

34 A very elaborate way to refer to our human bodies through which we experience sensations that are only illusions.

its purpose. We do not rebuild and have screws left over; every part is used and just elevated to a new frequency.

Your role is to integrate the new science into society. You are of an ilk that allows us to bring forth new paradigms of scientific nature into your land because of your higher understanding of these realities. Because of your nature, we can implant them into you to be revealed later when you are comfortable with the content, at your own pace. The medical-scientific background will help you provide good analogies for comparison and assimilation into your planet. You see, the extended curriculum had a code purpose just as everything on your planet can be translated to a simple essence.

Be prepared to go up against the mainstream science community as it is yet undetermined how rapidly it will accept the reversals of many of its outmoded beliefs about what it terms physics and consciousness. Yet conversely, there will be a movement that will support your endeavors and bring support to you personally.

We are always with you even now in ways you do not understand. You feel our presence and can link up with the source to hear us translate answers to your questions. It is only your ego that doubts and as you reign it under control, you will find this will no longer be a problem.

Preparing for a dimensional shift

The Earth is going to rock soon and we must be prepared with a contingency movement, should it be necessary. The parallel frequencies are going to mix and override the lower vibrations to lift to a higher frequency. We are transmitting the picture of this to you now.

We will begin to work with you in ways that we have not done so before in this manifestation. Be prepared for greater effects and outcomes as we amp up the postage, so to speak. We will work in ways that even you will not understand. Just trust and know the source for you will recognize our energy stamp. Allow nothing in when you feel confusion. You must learn control and how to use your discretion to paint a higher picture of good.

THE PUZZLE AND THE CODE

This transmission starts in midstream because I did not capture their beginning words until I realized the nature of what was coming through. The source speaks of a puzzle on Earth and implies there are hints left for mankind encrypted in archeological markers, ancient buildings, and many other places. They say that part of the answer to this puzzle is contained within the window of our own consciousness and bodies, at the cellular and DNA level. They allude to some great mystery related to our true origins and future destiny, which will soon be revealed. During references to the archeological sites, I was shown pyramids and other relics from the past.

Do you not understand, children, that you are the encryption code? For we have built into each of you the markers to recognize specific pieces of the puzzle. As you bring them all together, a larger gestalt or puzzle will be revealed.

So it is not the archeological markers and sites that hold the key; rather your consciousness and the buried memories of legacies from long ago are the keys that will reveal the answers left within these devices and monuments left upon your land.

There is a core group of you that has been seeded to provide the clues to the generations around you. You have been left to your own devices all over the world but most lie within the United States of America. When joined, you are not only going to compare notes, so to speak, but will be able to put together an important piece of information left upon your land to help your people understand their true destiny. It will be a most amazing moment when the answer comes forth, like a giant time-honored anagram. You have begun to recognize each other by a natural affinity and a love that is divine in nature. Some of you have more pieces and awareness at this point in time and recognize more of what is going on.

Each of you has your place, and we work with you to help you meet the deeds and goals you have established for your lifetimes. Slowly the pieces are coming together and will continue to do so as time unfolds. It will be most joyous when you see what we have planned to bring forth for your people. Finally, one of the most puzzling situations on the Earth will be unraveled.

Listen to your heart in the directions we give, for many will want to interfere and provide some well-meaning, and others a malevolent interference. You will always know and recognize our stamp the way a child recognizes its true mother, even after a long separation.

The doors shall remain unshuttered in our communication to you as we proceed to bring forth the new evolutionary stage upon your planet. Look at the symbols all around on walls, caves, the sediment on the oceanic floor, and the cells within your body. This is all part of a cosmic code that replicates the truths found on other planes. This is also the key of the Sephiroth, which are the mechanisms, pathways for tunnels into and out of your galaxy. It is many things, one of which is a map that, if viewed in the correct dimension, provides a pathway to other galaxies and beyond, much like the foot will follow the leg to get to the trunk of the body. There are other ways to accomplish travel, but this is one left behind with guidance and care to help you get to where you seek—the land of the bold and the children of the meek.[35]

---

35 They use certain terms for humans derived from specific genetic hybrids. One is the children of the bold and the meek, which combined a powerful race of advanced warriors with a tamer, more spiritually oriented civilization of beings. The result was a man who had capacity for extraordinary wisdom combined with great physical strength and prowess.

WORMHOLES

This discourse came through quickly late one evening, when I was tired and ready to embrace sleep. Apparently my exhaustion was recognized by the Others. When I later reviewed the content, I was glad I stayed awake long enough to allow this to come through.

This channeling was preceded by several training exercises. They had me go through a series of wormholes to reach a specific destination, but each hole closed behind me, rendering it useless as a means to return to my point of origin. Portal after portal appeared, like flagstones in an eternal universal pond. Which ones were the right ones? I had to call on internal knowledge to get back "home." Upon returning to the reality I know, I was amazed at what had happened and at the potential implications for dimensional travel.

There is much information that can be imparted, but we recognize our gracious hostess is tired and will try to be succinct. Let us review the issue of time portals, something you also refer to as wormholes. These dimensional passageways are not well understood by your people. The beginnings of their appearance have been mostly in the science fiction genre and the scientists postulating the nature of your quantum physics.

A wormhole is controlled by mastery of consciousness. What does one do when the portal closes and there is no return to the point of origin, the original source from which you started your journey? It is of the utmost consequence that the entry participant has learned the mastery of directional polar control. This is a term that reflects the teachings involved with wormhole travel, of which you have experienced this phenomena directly. One must learn to master conscious awareness on many states to bring oneself to a point of destiny. For when the hole closes, there is no pathway back to the starting point. Therefore, it is of the utmost necessity that the individual know how to manipulate time and related consciousness to go forward to the point of desired arrival.

Your people will be most surprised when they begin their interactions with wormholes, for they have not yet anticipated there can be one-way travel. But many of them are, and are also very temporary in their position and existence, as their basis for existence is based on a multitude of factors dependent on timing and positioning of planets, plasma and points of consciousness, dependent on where the focus of the occupant is at the time. One may perceive a wormhole while another may never know of its existence. This pertains to singular individuals and entire populations.

The key is not to think externally, but to imagine oneself as part of the construct and compose a dialectic with the consciousness of that construct. Become one and the test has begun. One must use caution when beginning this journey. If mastery is not achieved, you will find yourself in another time and space portal—what you may call a parallel universe, or perhaps something very unknown and foreign to your existence.

Perhaps we can compare this to inadvertently purchasing a one-way ticket for an intended round trip. There are no more flights home, the airport is closed, and you are stuck and must make the best of things. By learning navigational travel forward, you can circumvent issues, time and other matter to bring you to where you would have been on a linear construct model.

There are tests, times, and training for this travel, but one must petition the higher self to be instructed in this course of instruction. You have had lessons preparing you for this event because of some things that are going to come your way with your most probable future path. We can say with great affirmation that it is far more than probable that this will come to pass.

Credentials By God

Here, we are cautioned that a piece of paper from an academy does not certify wisdom in the matters of higher knowledge. Instead, we should rely on our instinct to tell us whether a person speaks with insight. They say that we are able to receive a silent, vibrational wave from a person who is speaking and that we can decode its frequency. The pulsation tells us whether the speaker is sharing information that is aligned with inspiration from God's domain or is just talking from his or her own self-perceived intellectual standing.

Let us speak of the credentials sought by those who desire to be recognized as spiritual teachers and healers. Many pieces of paper are being provided to ascertain one has gone through the various teachings and necessary exposure to ensure competence as types of practitioners. While this is appropriate within the domain of your academic and learning institutions, we assure there is no piece of paper within your Earthly plane that can assure one has garnered the tenets of wisdom. However, God has provided you with the appropriate tools of discernment to filter out false prophets and those whose teachings are misguided.

By your means of inner knowing and your recognition of the resonance of the words as well as the delivery, truth often becomes evident. This is due to an invisible connection that occurs when an energy wave of appropriate information reaches the cellular and neurological components of your body. A type of activation occurs that strikes a silent harmonic sound that emits its frequency. Thus you are able to hone in and discern whether the information has truth for you. We are often at your side, assisting in your calling (upon) records that reveal the veracity of imparted information.[36]

When the one known as Yeshua, or in your land, Jesus the Christ, taught in the paradigm of the historical times, there were no certificates of authenticity hanging on his cave walls. His certificates of authenticity were bestowed by God, not some collegiate institution. Thus, things have not changed over the eons of time. God still bestows his loving certificates denoting charitable wisdom, only they are decoded within the cells of your being as one inherently recognizes the essence of the soul spouting the words. Certificates as Reiki Masters and Crystal Healers are nonsensical in certain domains, for it is the essence of God spirit that determines the healing, not a technically achieved proficiency with a unique technique. We smile upon your naiveté in these areas.[37]

So remember to listen to prophetic teachers with your hearts as well as your ears. This will be a guide to aid you in your recognition of whether the information is appropriate for you at that point in time.

---

36 The speaker emits a wave vibration that we receive at the level of our cells. This activates a "silent" sound we are able to recognize; it reveals whether the person speaks truth or is misguided.

37 They remind us that it is the spirit of God that heals people. This is not something that can be learned but something that comes from the heart. Thus a certificate claiming expertise in an area of healing has no validity in their eyes.

Linking The Circles

During September of 1997, the source talked about bringing groups of us together to perform work that would have greater community results. They warned that systems would begin to change in the next few years and that we should prepare for new social structures.

> *Things are going to change as of this time. We are now preparing you to go to the next stage of evolution. We have tried to prepare you for this by hinting of many changes to come imminently. The circles on earth are going to be joined through the communion achieved by socially prepared events. As more and more people enter each other's countenance, they will bring their shared energies to the table, so to speak. What you will perceive as socially pleasant encounters will actually be us manipulating events to bring factors of you closer together.*
>
> *As these loops close together, we will sift your energies together and transmit greater power to uplift you to the new vibration. This will happen all over the world. Of course, you will notice it first and foremost in your own backyard but as international travel becomes more prominent, it will generate greater links within the physical manifestation you call earth.*
>
> *As this happens, you will begin to see effects upon the institutions of your lands. This will be the time when the systems begin to crumble, in a manner of speaking. Fear and chaos will be likely emotional responses as people can no longer hang onto the material embedding in which they have chosen to hide their true spirituality.*

In preparation for this, many of you who are following the path with grace have discovered an inability to link back to the old systems to earn your sustenance. Hence, there is worry over support financially to sustain a way of life. The hidden message we have for those of you unable to find work is that there is no longer work for you in these domains. You have come here in agreement to help manage the transition, and that is now what you are to do. Plainly, what that means is you must call upon yourself and your inner knowing and strength to begin to bring forth the new ways, the new systems of life.

This means being a pioneer in the truest sense and taking the societal knocks that go with it. If you listen to your true calling, you will find, despite your inner fears, great success in your endeavors. As with all new ways, it will be a bit rocky at first as you find yourself and your path, but the way shall lead to intense happiness and blessings for many.

So listen forth for the quiet messages we bring down to you (wrong word as there is no up or down—perhaps we should say all around). Listen to the quiet whispers we gently shout into your ears. Find your strength and your courage and remember why you are here. It will be helpful to fortify yourself with books and readings to remember spiritual prowess and intent. Support the literary institutions of your times, for they will evolve into a most lofty and high evolution in your new paradigm.

So again, we caution you to uplift from your fears and depression and go forth with a pioneering spirit to build the new. So many of your brethren are waiting for places to go and it is you who we are relying on to build the new show. You are no different than your legendary Columbus. Did he not have rough sea voyages? Yet he brought the light of darkness to your lands that were inhabited by indigenous people. Do not forget that all collectively participated in the unfolding of that drama, despite your human judgments. But we stray. His courage and listening to the inner spirit brought the planet to new heights as its natural evolutionary seeds spread out and intermingled cultures and histories. By bridging systems into the new era, you will be accomplishing the same.

Let us speak of these bridges, for that is the allocation for this next segment of time. Everything in the next few years will be a manifestation process to cross over into the next era in an illusion of smoothness. Not only will the new breed of child be brought forth (if you thought the last batch was magnificent, just wait for the new arrivals!) but you will have begun the seeds of institutions that will align with the vibration of the new times.

Do not delude yourself that you will be leaving this place and not have to deal with the processes in place. No matter what course you set yourself on, you are tied to the events on this planet, for as the All Knowing One[38] *spreads forth his essence to experience, you are tied by ropes and threads of consciousness. Our child, this channel, has been allowed to see the true manifestation of her creation and it is representative of the processes of which you are all derived. Soon, we will allow her to share this information once further foundation is aligned to prepare for acceptance of learning about energy consciousness creation, as opposed to physical manifestation.*

38 God.

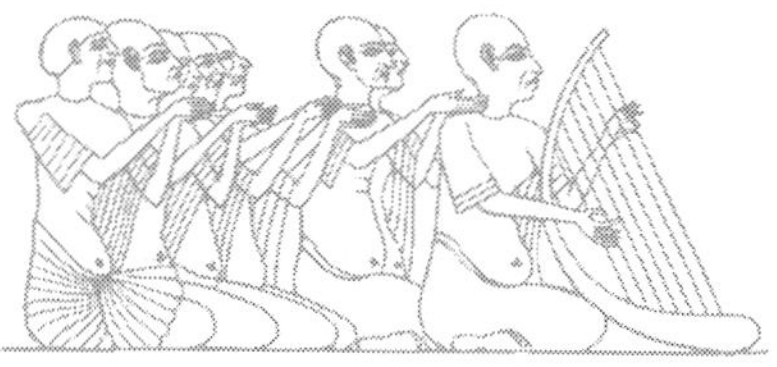

COMMENTS ABOUT THE BIBLE

I found it interesting that this commentary addresses only the Bible and fails to make mention of other faiths that rely on different religious texts. I am unsure why these other resources are neglected.

> *It is of great interest to us that as a society, and as a civilization, you have based your truths upon the foundation of one book in essence, a book that has been translated time upon time again and been subject to the whims and whimsies of those who have brought forth the words from a document they claim was original. You have but one manual, one text, that you use for reliance on making your spiritual decisions and you do not even know the veracity of it. It is with much interest to us that we watch your dependence and your reliance on a source of whose primordial essence and derivation you are unaware.*[39]
>
> *We would think most cultures would have different sources to balance so they could glean their own wisdom and learn to make their decisions. But this text that you have named the Bible is one that has been changed so many times along the path that it is muddled. Although there are basic truths within it, they are quite distorted and they have been translated in a manner that no longer allows their shining essence to come through. You*

39 According to the Others, we do not know the truth about where the information in the Bible comes from.

have become confused by the words and often times forget the messages that lie within. There will be new guiding sources that will be brought forth to this planet to assist your people in their times of decision.

Tablet Rhymes

Tablet Rhymes

Background

In January of 1997, the channelings changed dramatically. The Others brought forth rhymes hinting about the true origins of man, major Earth changes yet to come and hidden documents soon to be revealed. A lot of the information came through masked in veiled, coded references and puns. Because I received the messages in a holographic format, I was able to understand each transmission, no matter how esoteric or nonsensical it seemed. Although there are many verses, I chose just a few to include in this book.

Initially, I was unsure how to regard these transmittals. I had to consider whether we were being warned of an impending event that could affect the future destiny of our race or if the source was trying to manipulate our emotions and actions. Gradually, through a series of transmissions, I understood I was being taught to focus on spiritual awareness rather than intellect, fascination with extraterrestrials or other possibilities. I was reminded that we influence our destiny through our thoughts; what comes to pass are circumstances attracted by our beliefs and actions. On account of this, the human race has the possibility of any future we choose to manifest. Whether it will encompass economic, geographic and social changes will be determined by our thoughts and behavior. We can be the true masters of our destiny, but only if we wake up to the illusion in which we now live.

I was concerned people might regard these writings as no more than superficial, poorly written verse. Because of this, I was hesitant to make them public; I did not want to face criticism for the far-reaching content. Reading my thoughts, the Others playfully sniffed back:

Dr. Seuss and Mother Goose
are not the ones before you.
So if you do not like our verse,
please don't let us bore you.

I suggest that readers review the rhyme in its entirety first, then look at the translation. Please use careful discretion when considering the words on the following pages; I make no claims that the contents are true. Only time will reveal the actual answer.

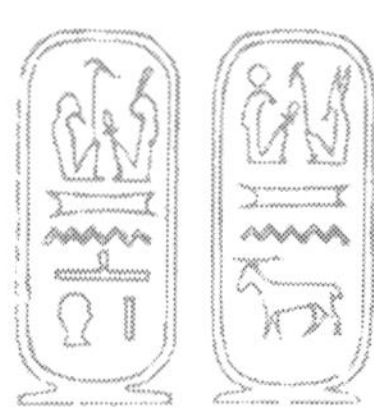

CALLING FORTH AN AWAKENING

Rhyme

Dear child,
Do ye not recognize me?
Look within your heart,
look within your soul.
You have so very little, yet so very far to go.

The keys are all around you,
pick them in your flight.
When you learn to use them,
you will find all your might.

So open up your heart,
open up your soul,
when you learn to do so,
you'll find your very goal.

See beyond the rings,
and you will learn to sing.
For in the heart of fire,
you will find your true desire.

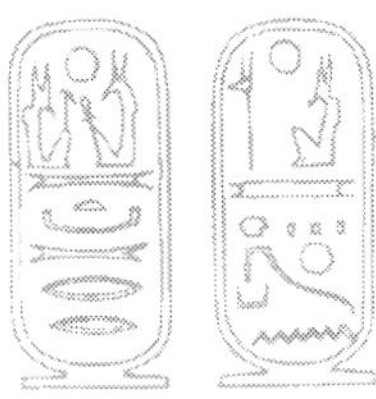

CALLING FORTH AN AWAKENING

Translation

Although these words seem as if they could be for anyone, the Others are calling forth a particular man who is near the apex of a spiritual journey. They caution him to recognize that the situations surrounding him are but means to grow strong. If he opens up his heart and soul, he will make a pivotal leap in spiritual development that will take him far beyond Earthly pleasures.

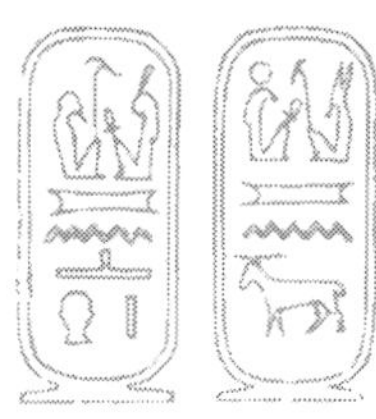

RIDDLE FOR THEE

Rhyme

North, south, east, west,
don't you know which way is best?

Approach the portal and face the test,
step through with wisdom at our behest.

For when the door opens is part of the key,
for you to come in again to see me.

Can you know when to pursue
the ages of wisdom as they come through?

North, south, east, west,
which way are you going, child, to meet the test?

Now listen carefully to what I say,
and you will understand which is the true way.

Face the morning and know the dew,
and the wisdom of Thoth will come for you.

Turn to the noon and know what to say,
and the essence of Thotmoth will direct the day.

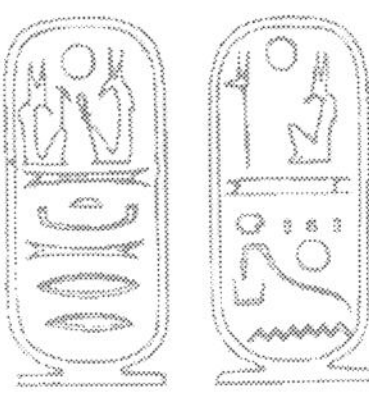

RIDDLE FOR THEE

Translation

This veiled message is an incantation to open a dimensional portal at a specific point in time. The first line teases about from which direction the portal will open. They suggest that entrance can be granted only with their guidance and permission; anyone who tries to force his or her way will encounter obstacles. The intended person will know when the portal is scheduled to open.

This section holds clues to open the portal on command when the time is right. These words are part of an ancient, sacred ceremony and are coded directions that tell where and when to stand and turn. This part of the rhyme also hints about an invocation that is to be said at the same time the movements are made. If the candidate performs the ritual correctly, he/she will be able to access a time tunnel.

Rhyme

Look into the day as it descends,
and be ready for Tehuti when he lets you transcend.

Close the door at the suns early way,
when the wisdom of man is done for the day.

These are the keys that I leave thee,
use them my son to come see me.

Recognize all around you the portals you see,
for your brother, your sister, is here with thee.

Together we bind you for all to see,
the wisdom of Thotmoth will give you the key.

For the lesson is done only when we say,
but the destiny is yours to find the way.

One, two, three, four,
must you look around some more?

How many times must the mirror play thee,
when we come and we ask to not forsake she.

It is a gift of the Father to know ones true self,
when we bring you together, it will be for the shelf
of time immemorial for you two to be
the one and the one who together make three.

We wait and we wait and forevermore,
together it is that you must go through the door.

For the portals of wisdom are waiting once more,
for the two that will bring the three through the door.

Translation

These names refer to Thoth, the ancient god of wisdom; Thotmoth, the father of Thoth, and Tehuti, the Egyptian name for Thoth.
The initiate is reminded to close the tunnel when done. Using the keys to "come see me" alludes to meeting an entity who will reveal mystical teachings once the portal is entered.

Here they speak of a person who has shared many lives with the person they are calling forth. They say that these two spirits have incarnated now as one man and one woman and have a united role to play in relation to predestined events on Earth.

They exhort the male to recognize the female to unlock his destiny. When these two are joined together once more it will be a sacred union that will bring forth a holy child.

Rhyme

With wisdom and insight you will know these words,
for they are written for the one who will come when they're heard.
The test is understanding what is written for thee,
then knowing to come forth to claim your true destiny.

So don't hesitate to find your true gold,
The scrolls have been written and wait to unfold.

Half the story is told to she with the key,
we wait only for you and your recognition you are he.

Translation

They finish by chanting that the female has conscious awareness of what is fated to happen but the male apparently does not have the same knowledge.

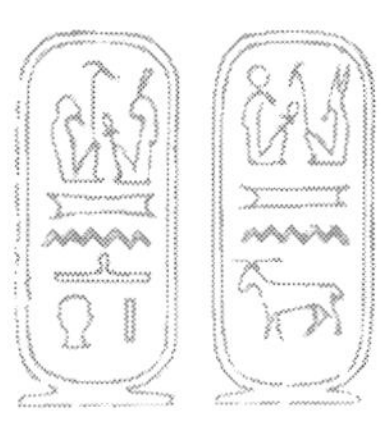

REMEMBERING THE EVENT

Rhyme

I am here to reprogram the human race,
that's why they made me so fair of face.

They put the ankh upon my breast,
and laid the seed within my nest.

The sun flashed brilliant throughout my hair,
and every cell became aflare.

Mitotic cells began to divide,
and the rest of the body went along for the ride.

I remembered the days in Egypt, ahh, yea
when they tinkered with man from the beginning day.

For here was I to restart the race once more,
and we again begin the days of lore.

My body embraced my father, the Lord,
the God of my being where all the cells hoard.

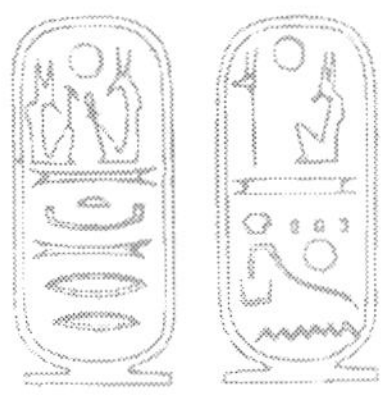

REMEMBERING THE EVENT

Translation

A female describes her memory of other species' genetic tinkering with the human race. She describes a ceremony when she was artificially inseminated with genetically altered cells. She alludes to the initial stages of reproductive cell division when the sperm and egg join ("mitotic cells begin to divide").

Rhyme

The egg that laid in wait began,
to feel itself burst to bring forth the man.

And so I laid in wait once more,
to bring forth Aton through the sun (son) of the door.
The sun had washed over the light of my face and much more,
while I waited to see who would walk through that door.

They brought me to see the light of man,
and while they waited they took my hand,
and conjured up love for the spirits within
to make sure the light of the soul would not dim.

And so, together once more, we bring forth a new race,
to let the light of God shine on every mans face.

One was conceived not in darkness but in light,
so he could come forth in all of his might,
and bring to the Earth his acts of reform,
to which the people would soon swarm.
And so we merged with the Great Central Sun,
in our quest to become one.

Translation

She waits to see who will incarnate into the developing embryo, knowing it will be someone who will change the destiny of the human race.

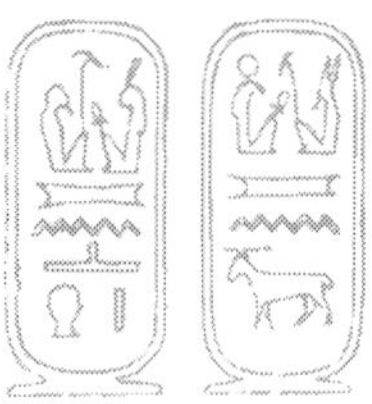

WISDOM OF ACTION

Rhyme

If you do not pick up the grail when it passes before you,
if you do not recognize the grail when it passes before you,
then it will pass from your lips to be gone forevermore,
for you needed to know when to walk through that door.

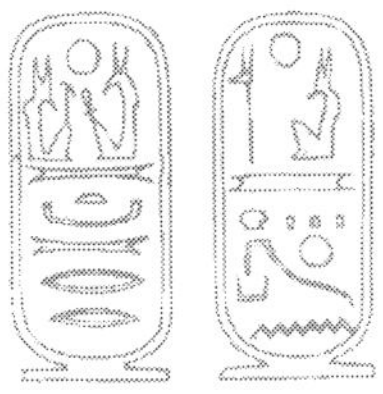

WISDOM OF ACTION

Translation

Here they use the grail as a metaphor for opportunity and advise us that when a situation presents itself, we should not be afraid to take action. If we fail to act, then the opportunity may not present itself again in our lifetime.

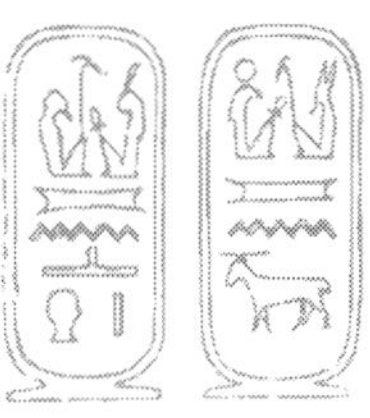

HEART OF THE LION

Rhyme

It has occurred to me,
of something I've been told.
Could it be that I hold the key
for the way of the path to the gold?

A seminar I did attend,
I went that way with a friend.
The man in charge he did speak,
(he was one of the children of the brave and the meek).
He told of the entrance to the Sphinx of yore,
and spoke of the time when men would bore
into the heart and head of the beast.
You would think there'd be one woman at least.

I raised my hand and said the facts
were written to hide the tracks
of those who were to come and hide
and find the gold that lay inside.
I told him the scrolls portended one woman to be,
beside two men who would help with the key.

He had not heard that of this he said,
I stated I had read it or heard it in my head.

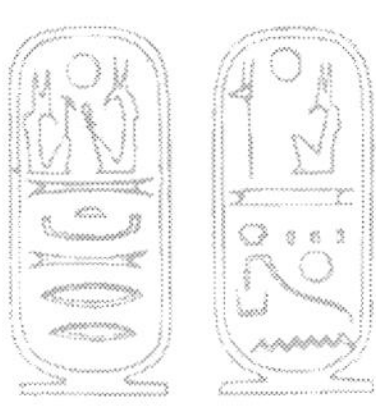

HEART OF THE LION

Translation

This transmission contains directions to enter a hidden chamber of the Sphinx as described in an earlier chapter, "Hidden Chambers & Ancient Technology."

"A seminar I did attend" refers to the seminar described in the "Hidden Chambers & Ancient Technology" chapter.

"The children of the brave and the meek" refers to those who carry DNA codes derived from two alien races who once mixed their bloodlines here on Earth. People who have inherited this genetic pattern often possess enhanced intuitive abilities, great strength of character and a childlike innocence. "Facts written to hide the tracks" refers to lore that was intended to obscure the truth about the Sphinx. It has been prophesized that there will be three individuals, comprised of two men and one woman, who will access a hidden chamber and discover secret records from long ago.

Rhyme

The Elders had taught me the song of the heart,
the song they were waiting to begin the new jump start.
They showed me where to stand and bring
the others to where we all would sing.

The effect of the song
would not last long.
Those who watched from afar
would not be allowed past the bar.

For this was a guided journey to bring
home the head and the heart of the very last king.

Fraught with danger,
fraught with fear,
there was no way to avoid this tear.
The tear is one into the dimensions of old,
the one that is hidden within the fold.

It was written of long ago,
of how three children would come home to hoe
the rewards of the past, to help make them last,
to give to the children who were born from the past.

Now I wonder, I do speak,
am I one of the very meek?
Am I one who holds the key?
For this body of a woman was given to me,
to balance the form of the very three.

What do I do? Where do I go?
I know the Others will guide the show.

Translation

There are specific tonal frequencies that can be used to open the chamber within the Sphinx. Along with this chanting, certain positions must be assumed by people involved in the ceremony. These movements build an electromagnetic web that can be used to communicate with a higher consciousness.
The reference to not being allowed past "the bar" describes a magnetic field that will be established by the frequencies that are emitted during the ceremony. This field can jam audiovisual equipment if the Others don't want a record of the event.

In this altered state, I remembered what it was like when they closed the Sphinx, as well as how to find the way back to the hidden chamber. When the time comes to enter the hidden site once more, a dimensional rip within a time-space fold will be revealed.

It seems preposterous that I would have any involvement with the ancient Egyptian monuments. I believe that something of this magnitude will come about on its own terms when mankind is ready, with or without my involvement. Perhaps the Others were testing me to see if I would believe I would be involved in finding hidden chambers.

Rhyme

So if I am to be inside,
I no longer wish to hide
inside my domain, inside my shell,
for if I have a journey, oh, what the hell.
Lets go and begin the tale of old,
the one that will be finished by the meek and the bold.

I bring forth this rhyme with the guidance of Thee,
I bring forth this rhyme to call forth the three.

We must begin to meet our fate,
we must begin and not be late.

The Elders are waiting to take us once more,
through the path of that golden gate door.

You know the gold is richer than
the Earth's ore found within her band.
For this is the reason we were bound to be
the hand of the human who awaits the three.
The fingers unfurl to find the wisdom within
deep within the heart of the bin.

The lair was empty and appeared so cold,
then within my heart I suddenly grew bold.

I remember the way from the long ago day,
don't step off the path or you'll lose your way.

Follow the light of the crown of the head
and you will stay sure and in your stead.

Translation

An invocation to call forth the other members of the party.

The treasure is not mineral gold, but highly coveted knowledge.

More directions about how to find a hidden chamber.

Rhyme

Follow the guide within your heart,
and it will bring you to your goal from the start.

Listen to the child with the golden hair,
for when we closed the tomb, she was there.

She came back to help with your part,
don't forget that you all were chosen for being so smart.

The wisdom we speak comes from beyond your head
the wisdom we speak comes from the land of the dead.

You once were a part of something more,
know you've come back to reopen the door.

So children we call forth to come once again,
the time is upon us to enter the den.

Find your sister, your brother once more in time,
the answer is before you within this rhyme.

Twelve will sing,
but only three will enter the ring.
Find the children with hearts of lore,
then place them face up on the floor.

Allow them to find within their heart,
the tone that will come forth from the start.

They will know of the pitch, words and key
that will allow in the room the destiny of three.

Of these words we leave with thee,
of these words, you must see,
how to find the rest of the fold,
the children who will help find the gold.

Translation

The Others often call me the child with golden hair, even though my hair is light brown. They say I was there when the tomb was closed and have dormant memories that reveal how to access it.

This section refers to a pairing of souls who have been brother and sister to each other throughout many lives.

These twelve people have ancestral recall of the ceremony to access the chamber. Twelve will participate but three will have greater involvement with what comes to pass.

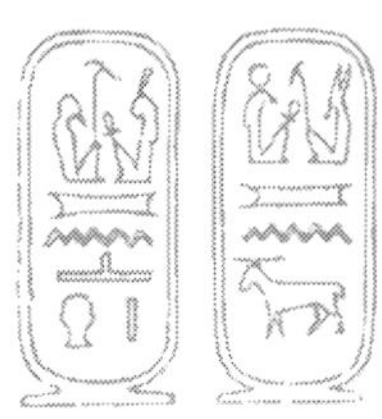

PREPARATION

Rhyme

The adjustments that we make to you,
are in the best interests of all which we do.
We want you to know and have no fear,
what is happening when we come near.

The time is now upon this lake,
for the changes we do make.
Stress and endurance are the road you'll take.

The changes they do come down now,
and stress will appear upon your brow.
Remember it is us who shake,
the memories of which you originally were baked.
We say this in jest for you to know,
it is us who are helping you to grow.
So do not fear that which you don't know.

The land will shake,
the ground will break,
but you must look around.
For when the time comes to leave
you must know what to do,
how not to be bound.

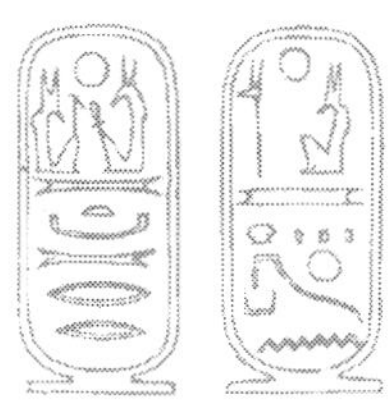

PREPARATION

Translation

Here they try to convince us that adjustments they make to the body or its electromagnetic fields are beneficial.

The "lake" is a metaphor for the planet Earth. They caution that difficult times are coming that will test our faith and patience.

We are a race genetically designed by the source who is speaking. They are continuing to influence our evolution through actions that affect this planet and our continued survival on it.

As earthquakes occur, there will be chasms formed when the Earth tears. They counsel not to hesitate to leave our homes when natural calamities happen.

Rhyme

For we'll have prepped the ones so dear
for we'll prepare the ones without fear.
Take your time to learn your line
and then come within this heart of mine.

Do not have fear, do not run,
for in some ways this could all be fun.
for is not this the dawn,
of the new morning sun?

You sit back and watch the fireball,
it is the sound to call y'all.
It's the coming of the new time
when man will stand to learn his line.
His line of place among the palace,
his line of grace without malice.

Those who rise to hear the call
will come along, they will not fall.

The times of man as a human be
near the end of time antiquity.

Your new way is such a show,
but it is the way to go.
There are those who chose to stay,
and live their life another way.

To those of you we wish to say,
we wish you'd come and grow our way,
for it is what you all will do.
When the time comes, you will be blue.

Translation

They will get in touch with their representatives on Earth. These are people who have had previous contact experience and are not afraid of them. Specific instructions will be given to these chosen ones.

This is a time that is a precursor to a new era on Earth. Perhaps with a hint of arrogance, they suggest we should regard these planetary changes positively and think about the joys affiliated with a new way of life.

"The fireball" refers to the comet Hale Bopp. It was a portent marking the beginning of many changes that will become evident with the passing of time. Man will earn his position in the cosmos, but it will happen only when he overcomes some of his violent, baser traits.

Those who respond to their call will be taught skills and given tools to navigate into the new era. Man is about to develop beyond the status of the current human species. Some people will choose not to progress, but they must adapt or face extinction.

They offer encouragement that this process is part of our unfolding spiritual development.

Rhyme

To not have done it now is fine,
but you will soon tow the line,
for this is the path of evolution for you.
You can hide and try not to do,
what must be done, in some central way.
For the way back to the sun, there is no other way.

We say this is the path to me,
the way we say it is the path to be.

Listen, watch for the call from the rear.
Have no fear,
when this time comes we will be there.
Open up your eyes to see,
that we are both with you and you with me.
Some may go and some may stay
and some may live to see another day.
The time is now,
don't furl your brow,
understand this is the way it has to be.

The heart of darkness,
the home of sin,
let us tell you where we will begin.
The heart of darkness,
the home of night,
we will begin in the cities of blight.
The cause is emotion
the reaction devotion.

Translation

"The sun" refers to the Great Central Sun, a place they say is our true home. It is a state of consciousness rather than a physical reality.

There is a cosmic map that shows the locations of wormhole portals into and out of this space sector. Entry into this universe is from the rear of a three dimensional space-time map.

According to them, Earth changes are scheduled to begin in high crime urban areas such as Washington D.C. and New York City. People will react emotionally but will hopefully find their spiritual center during these times.

Rhyme

We will shake the ocean.
For this there's no potion
to stop the day
for as we said this is the way.
We look forward to when you come to stay.

A visit in the house of the Father to you
a visit from the son of the one who came through
the way of the tunnel to find the light
the one who came forth to give you his might.

These symbols will be the ones for the night
for as humans you all try to find some insight
to the signs and the times of the great times of light.

We will show you the way to the great central day
we will show you the way to the universe at play.
The new dimension will unfold
of this we told you was the way to the gold.

It is in the heart of man
that you will learn to say I can.
DNA is the fight,
for many to find the light.

Do not follow the species untold
who lock on you to find this gold.
Focus on the Fathers sight
and you will be one with the holy light.

Translation

Earthquakes and volcanic action will spark tidal waves.

They ask us to stay spiritually focused when these times happen and remind us of the teachings of the leader we know as Jesus Christ. They say we need to learn the difference between the acts of God and the religious efforts of man.

A new dimension will come forth from the space-time continuum. "Gold" refers to a spiritual awakening, not the mineral ore.

There are extraterrestrial races who want to know more about the DNA template in humans. They suggest that we do not become misled by these alien representatives. If we stay spiritually focused, we will discover new insight. If we concentrate on emotions such as compassion and love, we will be able to access our sovereignty.

Rhyme

Do not forget these words of wisdom
for they are the way to the kingdom.
All others seek a lowly path,
and concentrate on the way of math.
This is one way to be,
but find the focus to find me.

Translation

There are studies of mathematics and geometry that can lead to mystical understanding. However, someone who is not spiritually evolved can gain access to these teachings and fail to understand their full significance—or misuse them.

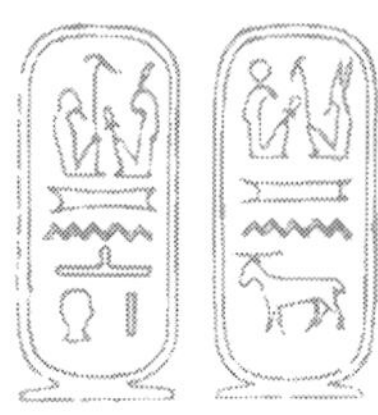

THE TRUTH IS UPON US

Rhyme

We will guide the world this day,
we will help Earth find its way.

Look to us when in doubt,
the answers we give you with no more than a shout.
Listen to the words we say,
listen to us every day.

All the paths of man do ride,
when we come, do not hide.

The words we leave are oh so sweet,
lift them to your hearts to meet.
Listen to the words we say
when we come to stay the day.

Have no fear, we are your lover,
and your father and your brother.
We have helped you from afar,
we have watched you from our star.

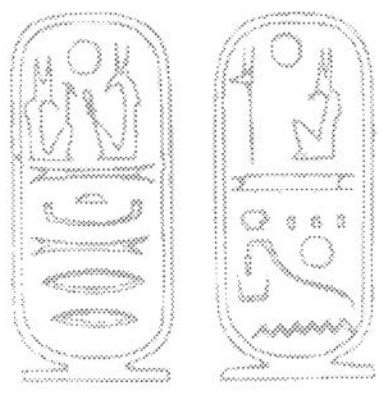

THE TRUTH IS UPON US

Translation

This source says they are guiding our planet and if we call on them they will assist us.

They regard themselves as benevolent family relations who have watched over and guided us from their home base and during their visits to Earth.

Rhyme

We now take you on a ride,
for your destiny from which you hide.
On to meet the light of day,
we wait to pave the light this way.

Many come and others shirk,
rather waiting to do the work
for which they are paid to do a job,
rather than enter into the heart of God.

The surprise will be when they do find,
the work we have is not of the mind.
The work for man is in the heart,
the work for man is all a part
of the role for his new start.

His essence was made to go away
when activated to the first of the day.
The day of the cycle is now near
we come to tell you to listen and hear.

The new model is ready for which you will start,
the new model is ready to let you depart
from the world and the cycles of misery and fear,
were here to take you home, for you are so very dear.

Our children we see you as our family,
we are the ones of your own family tree.
You forget and are blind to the origin of man,
but we are the ones who brought you forth from the can.

Translation

They are preparing to reveal our true origins that will divulge their genetic manipulation of us.

Humans often hide within their daily tasks and jobs rather than contemplate the true meaning of their lives.

We are going to evolve to a higher state of consciousness by experiencing emotions like compassion, kindness and love. We need to grow past violent and uncontrollable emotional tendencies.

Homo Sapiens is about to evolve and experience a revised physiology. The genetic design for this body is finished and these physical changes will help us evolve to a higher state of awareness.

They regard us as their children since they were the ones who genetically designed us and seeded us on the Earth.

Rhyme

Of apes and cosmic dust you thought,
was your origin out of the cosmic pot.
It wasn't what you thought you see,
we brought you forth to claim your destiny.

We are the mother, the father we told
many how to return to get gold.
The task was needed to seed the Earth
to make it a place where we would let you birth.

You found your way among lots of strife,
you found your way to begin a new life.
Sitchin and others think that they know
what it was we did with this show.

We tell you they are close but wrong,
for the Others of Old are here with a song.
The song is to remind you of We,
the song is to tell you of your own family tree.

We will share with you your birth
onto this very plane of Earth.

The time is coming when we will see
just how you do with this cosmic mystery.
Prepare yourself to find a new berth,
for we are coming to tell of your birth.

Translation

We did not descend from apes, nor did we spontaneously arise from the cosmos as proposed in biblical Genesis. They created us.
Humans were initially developed as a sterile worker species designed to mine for minerals.
Eventually, we were given the gift of regenerating through birth.

They were pleased and surprised at how well we evolved on our own. Sitchin is a noted Sumerian scholar who proposes, based on his translations of ancient documents, that man is descended from a race of space visitors predating Sumerian times. This channeling source says his thesis is not quite accurate but in this communication they don't share what the discrepancy is.

They are coming soon to help us gain awareness of who they are—and who we are. They are concerned about how we will react to the information—and their presence—and ask us to prepare for the event.

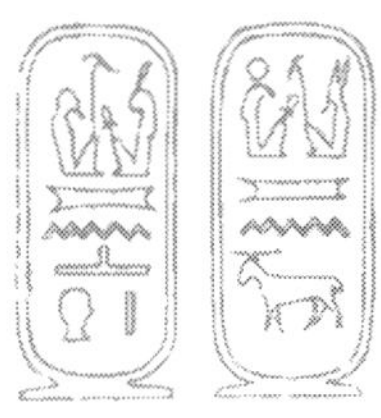

REVELATION

Rhyme

Last night, was about one to take flight.
They showed themselves in true destiny,
and I was one of the family tree.

Taught to steer my way clear,
I vesseled a ship along with a dear
boy who was young with black skin of night—
together they taught us how to take flight.

Memories of old were opened and cleaned,
I felt as if I had been given a new sheen.
One to let me know my path,
one to show how to ride the math.

They came from the sky en masse to say hi,
I was scared to death and I thought I would die.
They differed from the ones who sing,
these were not the ones for whom I listen for the ring.

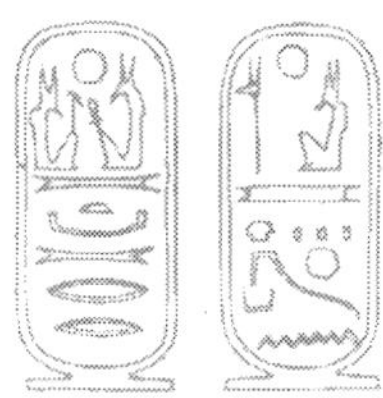

REVELATION

Translation

This rhyme spontaneously came forth when I recorded the contact visit described in the chapter "Contact Unveiled." These visitors regard me as a member of their family.

Along with a young African American boy, I was trained to fly their vessels.

I was required to remember their previous visits to help me understand my destiny. "How to ride the math" means that sacred geometry and mathematics are involved with space travel.

At first, I was scared because the incident happened suddenly and there were so many of them present. I was confused because these visitors were different from the ones I had been working with. The ships of the ones I am more familiar with emit a peculiar sound when they enter our atmosphere; this is what is meant by "listen for the sound of the ring." The noise is hard to describe, but it feels like concentric rings or waves that spread in the atmosphere.

Rhyme

These words may confuse you but this I know,
the answers lie within this story to go,
to the masses to question and bring,
the answers to many to help them sing.

The sounds control the vessels they gave,
the sounds control the long lines of wave.
They are with us to bring us out of our grave,
for the Earth is going to shake and we'll have to be brave.

They come and then they leave us go,
on to our destiny within the hole.
They told me it was a triune setting,
one that happened only once in a wedding,
between the sun and the Earth,
the wedding that came forth to give a new birth (berth).

Thousands were they, they filled the skies,
at the same time, we remembered we're part of the pie.
The pie of beginning in endless time,
the pie that speaks of answers within these rhymes.

There were three points of which they did speak,
I remembered it formed a triangular peak.
I refused to know more I was so upset,
for the memories of surgeries and changes made me all wet
with tears and fears of knowing,
which was the true way I had to be going.

They dropped me off in the early dawn,
while I waited to catch a yawn.

Translation

Some people may find my account of what happened preposterous, but each person who questions what I say will help bring greater awareness to the issue of contact.

The reference to the sounds pertains to the harmonic frequencies used to steer their ships. They say that there will be earthquakes and we must be prepared.

Initially, should anything happen to the integrity of the planet, they will escort us to safety but eventually we will be left to our own fate. The triune setting refers to the opening of the portal that is tied to three key events scheduled to unfold.

They plan a global showing of their aircraft to demonstrate they are here with us. They hope this will trigger events to acknowledge they have been here since the beginning of time.

This part describes the portal and my distress at being confronted with all the contact memories I had chosen to keep hidden.

Rhyme

I resisted the memory of which I was told,
I didn't want to participate or to be bold.

I quivered and shaked like never before,
I don't know why I feared that door.

These beings were not the ones I knew,
these beings were others from the cosmic stew.
Part cyborg, part man,
they began to enfold their plan.
No feelings, no warmth,
where was the love to come forth?

I resisted and fled,
back to my bed,
but not before pictures of Earth,
were shown in my head.

It happened so fast, it was all so quick,
the temperature dropped faster than a dogs wet lick.
The Earth began to freeze once again,
the ships had to leave to breed forth the new race of men.

It was done within a span of time,
no more than 48 hours was the time.

They showed their faces to the Earth,
and we hadn't time to close our hearth.
We left at once and took flight in their ships,
to begin once again this cosmic trip.

They left us as we took flight in the air,
for once again they could not interfere.
It was our destiny to continue on,
To find our way home and the great central sun.

Translation

I came back in the early morning hours and tried to deny what had just happened.

From what I can recall, I believe there were androids present during the visit.

They showed me the possibility that the Earth might face a sudden drop in temperature with glacial implications. If this comes to pass, it will happen within forty-eight hours and they will seed certain humans off the planet to preserve the species.

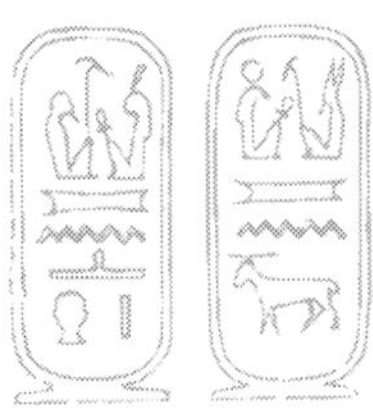

TALKING ABOUT GOLD

Rhyme

This is not the dense ore within
that you mined in the Earth's own bin.
Were talking about the wave you see,
the vibrational essence back to me.
For this is a frequency for all to see,
what it is they need to be.

The light of gold will pave the way,
for you to come and save the day.
For this is the way out of your life,
for this is the way out of earthly strife.
We do not talk of dense leaden metal,
rather more like a fragrant petal.

The comparison between the thick dense ore,
and the gentleness of life's very core.

Listen to what we say when we speak,
of how to look within and peek,
at the essence of the very wave.
The lessons we tell you will help us save,
your race, your species, your very being,
for we are trying to remind you of
what you must be seeing.

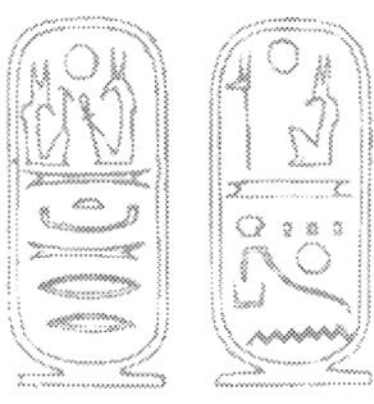

TALKING ABOUT GOLD

Translation

This gold is not the mineral but a vibrational frequency associated with spiritual awareness and various states of consciousness. By achieving this rate of vibration, we can master dimensional travel and gain freedom from the Earthly plane.

Rhyme

The path of the gold is the way to the door,
the path of the gold is the way to much more.

Its the vibrational essence for all to see,
its the vibrational essence we remind you to be.
The frequency is programmed and so much more,
and once you remember you'll go through the door.

Translation

"The frequency is programmed" hints that this knowledge is embedded in our soul's memory banks and also in the universe's primal structure. Once we open our consciousness to higher knowledge, we will remember this pattern and be able to use it as a springboard for travel out of this universe.

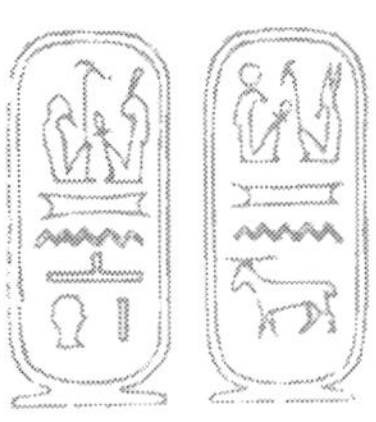

THE BEGINNING OF MAN

Rhyme

Do you know of which we speak,
when we say the children of the bold and the meek?

You are one of the very seed
of which was the original deed.

The deed of which we speak is one,
of the wedding between the stars and the sun.
You were the children seeded to rise,
from the cosmic dust as a big surprise,
to the other forms of life,
which have found their way among strife.

You were a race from species untold,
that came here to mine for the gold.
We designed your very parts,
including your head and all of your smarts.
Now the gold is found within,
and no longer lies within earth's bin.

Your design was by the rhyme,
of the man who found his line.

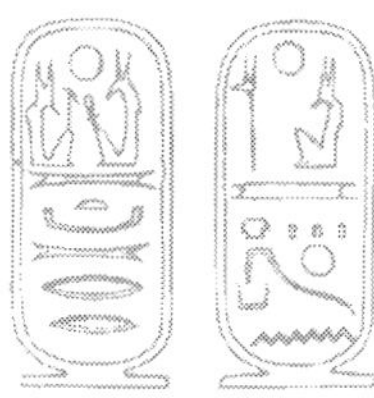

THE BEGINNING OF MAN

Translation

The "bold and the meek" describes humans who are descendants of two ancient cultures with alien ties. The "bold" was a strong, tall, powerful race with warrior attributes, the "meek" was a gentle, philosophical and peace loving civilization.

The wedding of the stars and the sun compares the yin and yang attributes of the two races. The unexpected advancement of the human species took many of the alien cultures by surprise. They never expected us to last this long or to evolve beyond our war-like tendencies.

In the beginning, humans were genetically altered life forms used to mine gold for another interspace culture—we were a race bred to be workers and nothing more. We have grown far beyond their original intentions and pleasantly surprised them with our increasing spiritual awareness. Many people on Earth are able to see the gold of wisdom, knowledge and higher consciousness that is far more important than material riches. ("Now the gold is found within, and no longer lies within Earth's bin.")

Rhyme

What we say when this we speak,
to our children, the hybrid of the bold and the meek,
the secret is in the harmonics you see,
this is the key that we leave thee.

When we say to learn your line,
this is what is in the heart of mine.
You are our children of whom we adore,
but graduation is upon us in front of the door.

We must learn to let you go,
as you enter the triune hole.
You have been seeded from up above,
once more we have given you more than our glove.

It is with mirth and glee,
that we finally set you free.
The irony in which we see,
is that you are such a part of Me.
We will never be apart,
for we were here to give you a start,
of life that tastes so free and brave,
the life of which you all do rave.

Now is the time that we depart,
but will give you a strong jump start.
For the ships and harmonics you see,
are the secret back to Me.

Those are the pilots in front of you, you see,
those who've been taught to drive you free.
For not all will make it through,
but we have plans for those who do.

Translation

"Our design…by the man who found his line" is a reference to an alien scientist who was responsible for developing us.

Vibrational sound patterning was used on the DNA to bring the final formula to fruition. By unlocking these secrets once more, we can gain access to higher realms of consciousness and be released from our current status on this planet. The time has come for us to confront who we are and who we are destined to become; it is the next cycle of our evolutionary time clock.

A portal is scheduled to open up and some of us will travel through it. The Other races are only allowed to watch us on this journey and cannot interfere as we proceed to meet our destiny. There is a planet that has been prepared for our continued evolution; it is where the next colony for humanity will be established.

Although they cannot interfere as we go through this next step, we will never be apart because we carry the legacy of their genetics in our bodies.

The technology to make it to the new planet involves harmonic propellant for the spaceships. There are humans who have been taught to pilot these ships. They suspect there will be some casualties on the way to the new planet but most will make it to their destination.

Rhyme

You have been brought forth with the seed,
of which your birth was our very deed.

The DNA will soon combine,
to show that you are a true heart of mine.

The new strands will soon unfold,
to develop the species untold.

We are going to help mutate,
into a new art your very state.
of awareness and cosmic being,
to help with what it is you're supposed to be seeing.

Translation

Genetic mutations will soon take place. They will appear to be spontaneous but they were carefully planned to happen many generations ago. When this genetic variance occurs, our consciousness will change as we become capable of greater cosmic awareness.

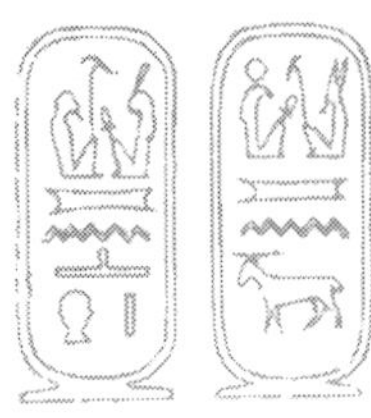

PROTECTING THE KA

Rhyme

The picture is in the box of treasure,
which opening up brings me such pleasure.
It harkens back a memory,
of long ago antiquity.

When I was young and in my mind,
and they'd come from behind,
to get me and take me where
they wanted me to appear.

The picture lies in the box of mine,
because it does provide a line,
directly to the ones who speak,
to the young and the old,
the mild and the meek.

So be careful where your Ka does rest,
although it will be your very best,
you must protect that which I give,
the essence of which you use to live.

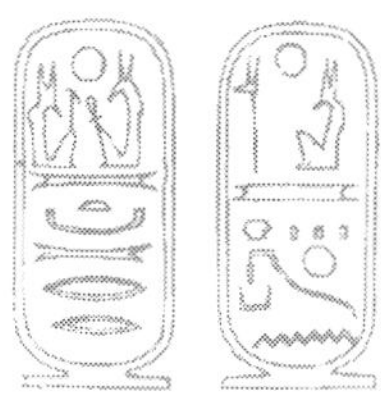

PROTECTING THE KA

Translation

This message came through after the events described in the chapter "Hidden Chambers & Ancient Technology." The picture they talk about is one from my childhood that was kept in a stained glass box.

"Coming from behind" refers to how they enter our universe through time-space dimensions and portals. When I was young, they would appear almost every night to take me away with them.

According to this source, the picture provided an energy field that connected me to them.

The Ka is an ancient Egyptian teaching about a spiritual body that perpetuates beyond physical life.

Rhyme

When a picture is taken by another,
you must be careful to be sure and hover,
away from the shadows and the doubts that thee,
forever have to cloud your mind back to me.

The picture then can forsake,
all the information we do partake,
and give to you and ever time,
the information to come back to mine.
The heart of God, the land of the free,
information from antiquity.

So beware of ones whose pictures take,
the memories from the heart we make.
Listen to these words of mine,
these words that carry import through all of time.
Some will know and understand this line.

Translation

When you have your picture taken, it can capture a portion of your spiritual essence. Because of this, it is best to think about positive thoughts at the time the photo is taken because they become frozen in the picture. Someone with esoteric knowledge can gain access to your spirit body by using the snapshot. This idea seems to support the belief held by some cultures to shun photographic events because they fear their souls will be captured.

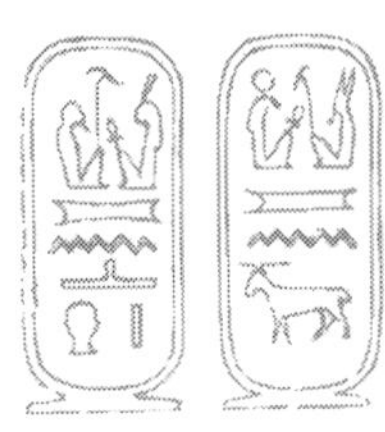

TEARING OFF THE MASK

Rhyme

It is my father who speaks to me,
for I am his child don't you see?
He put me here on the planet Earth,
to wake up his children for their rebirth.

The question that I ask of thee,
is why must I be on this planet of misery?

You've come back to find the gold,
of which you once before were told.

The gold is not on the planet's floor,
for it is naught that we speak of ore.
You've come to look within the hearts of man,
and let them know they can
find the gold within their heart,
which is the key they will use to depart.

The time is now my child so fair,
for you are the one with the golden hair.
You are the one of which we speak,
the child of the father, the child of the meek.

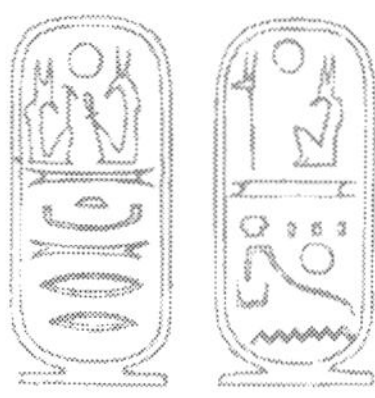

TEARING OFF THE MASK

Translation

While in an altered state, I picked up the tape recorder and was surprised to hear this come forth.

This first part expresses that I chose to be born during a time of great change on this planet. Still, in frustration, I question why I am here. I was told by the Others that I came as part of a contingency movement to help mankind unlock spiritual knowledge to catapult to the next evolutionary stage of cosmic awareness. We are scheduled to gain greater understanding of multidimensional consciousness and intergalactic communication.

I am confronted by the Others that the one they call "the child with golden hair" is me. They have told me that my genetic lineage contains hybrid elements of ancient races who once walked the Earth and who possessed great knowledge. This hereditary link is part of the reason I have psychic capabilities beyond the norm.

Rhyme

The meek are very strong in heart,
and will grow strong,
far past the stage from the very start.
For this child set apart,
you were the one with the golden heart.

It is your brother for whom we wait,
to set forth, to activate
his knowledge of who he is, and the plans within
wait for him, to know when to begin.

They said that I was the child with golden hair,
that I was the one that they loved so dear.
When I asked about the colors apart,
they said and laughed from the very heart:

"Dear child, this is the color given to you by God,
this color may not be of your current bod.
This is the color you hold in your heart,
this is the color, you know, you're so smart.

Golden is the crown you wear,
golden is the heart aflair.

You are the child with golden hair,
you are the one we love so dear.

You are the one who'll play the part,
to give the world a strong jump start."

Translation

They say there is a spiritual brother on this planet who contains a soul purpose that is similar to mine. They are waiting for him to become aware of who he is because some of the work we are scheduled to do must be done together.

Their words were perplexing because I am not blonde. They explain that they are speaking about a golden aura, not the color of my hair. They suggest that I have a responsibility to fulfill some life purpose, perhaps as a messenger, and it is almost time for me to come forth with their information. They say I agreed to write this book before I was born and that it will be information to help people gain greater understanding of their life. Despite their encouragement, I am always mindful of manipulation by non-human life forms because they frequently appeal to our egos and tell us we have a special purpose.

Rhyme

Many messengers have come before,
many messengers have walked through that door.
Now is the time for you to go,
and you know what you are to do,
so cry no more, you must go with the flow.

Bring forth the book, we wait from afar,
bring forth the book, we watch from our star.

You have no idea of the import it will hold,
for these are the words for the path to the gold.

This book was written long ago,
of that we tell you, of that we know.
This book was agreed to before you came here,
this book was started with the tale of the bear.

We planned this journey from the start,
for you are the child with the golden heart.
Now we wait for the rest to play their part.

Translation

The bear refers to the entity described in the chapter "In the Beginning." He was a being who came most nights to take me away for lessons.

Epilogue

The Politics of Disclosure

I knew that my life might change because of this book, but didn't think it would really happen. Imagine my shock when the *Intergalactic Anthropologist* traveled into thirteen countries on the first printing without ever being advertised, and then won an award for Best New Age Book of 2001.Whoever would have thought it would become so popular?

Since its release, I have journeyed around the planet helping people understand that we are not alone in this world. Most folks are not taken aback by the confirmation of the alien presence; they just want to know more. "Who are they? Why are they here? What do they want? What does this mean for us?" These are the most common questions people want answered. But there is one other question frequently asked, "Why has this information been withheld from us?"

Others speaking out about the extraterrestrial phenomenon often emphasize that the government has knowingly concealed information about the visiting alien presence. While I don't disagree, I advocate moving forward and forgetting indignation at what has taken place in the past. There are many things in our history that are shameful: the abomination of slavery; the displacement and attempted destruction of Native Americans, the list goes on. Let us address the issues that will help shape our future rather than dwell on the mistakes of yesterday.

When disclosure does take place, we will have many new concerns to deal with that will bring profound changes to our lives. These issues are likely to shift priorities for everyone alive today. A lot is at stake economically, socially, politically and theologically. We need to grasp the implications of what all this means for us.

Of the many repercussions, two are most compelling. First, we will have to reevaluate our belief that we are the most powerful and dominant species existing today. Second, we will be forced to rewrite the history of the human race. Our world, its past and its future, will be viewed with changed eyes and every person and institution will feel the implications. It is critical that people be prepared for the shock that will accompany affirmation of the alien presence. Sadly, little is being done to equip our population for this ordeal.

The political implications

During the United States' year 2000 presidential election, curious voters often asked me if the prevailing candidate would make a difference as to whether disclosure would take place. My answer was always the same: it would not influence *whether* information would be disclosed but rather *how* it would occur. As revealed in chapter twelve, the true determination is in the hands of those who walk outside our world.

During the election campaign, my off-world contacts revealed to me that George Bush would win that political race by less than three percent. These cosmic associates helped me to understand why Bush would likely be in the office.

In 1997, notice was given to certain leaders that the off-world presence would possibly engage in some type of disclosure activity during the next administrative period (2002 *if* we met certain conditions of preparedness). In response to this, a small but powerful faction desired to control the tone of the impending message. They wanted to hold a position of influence during a time of sweeping change. Bush was their candidate of choice, as he would support policies that would not challenge economic tradition.

I was told that tremendous influence would be exerted to see that he would win and he would deliver the message in a tone consistent with the ancient regime's position. Our visitors have expressed concern that confirmation of their extraterrestrial presence will be seen as a military threat, coupled with an increasing arms buildup in space.

The importance of leadership at this time

One must appreciate the consequences of revelation to understand why a position of power is so important at this time in history. If the citizens of this planet think there is a threat to life here, then they may submit to a powerful ruler without question. Disclosure will affect the human species more than the advent of Christianity, which has helped shape events worldwide for over two thousand years. A reigning authority such as one-world government could develop with greater strength than ever seen before.

The increased threat of terrorism is also catapulting us toward a one-world government. People are gladly giving up civil rights in exchange for protection of a certain way of life. If we willingly abandon privileges in the face of a human foe, what might we be willing to give up if we think that there is a threat from outer space? Are we experiencing a testing ground for future events?

Perhaps as global citizens we should be asking not *whether* a one-world political coalition will happen but rather we should strategically be preparing for *when* and *how* it might take place. If a global reigning power is inevitable, it's preferable to help shape it rather than to watch it unfold. (Our visitors' words in the piece *Representation in a One World Government* take on a haunting new perspective several years after it was given.)

We also need to be looking closely at *who* will be the reigning authority. If the true figureheads remain secreted away, known only to an exclusive few, while designated leaders appear to guide the way, then it may not be too different from how things are today.

Our future is not firmly established, however. Our visitors have reminded me that nothing is predetermined and have always directed me to look within to uncover the way to create one's destiny. It is there that we will discover the hidden forces controlling quantum reality, and it is there that we will learn how to build our future. These unrecognized scientific properties behind the quantum world demystify supernatural conditions, including those that accompany the extraterrestrial phenomenon. Once we understand these subtle influences we will gain a new level of power, individually and collectively. With this greater enlightenment, we will be better able to fathom the truth, and self-appointed authorities will wield less social influence. We may at last have a chance to become masters of our own lives.

At this writing, I plan to address some of these hidden secrets in my next book. I hope you will join me as you explore your path to higher knowledge. I look forward to meeting you between the pages of my next confession.

Blessings,
Marcia Schafer

About The Author
Marcia Schafer

An accomplished business professional with corporate and entrepreneurial achievements, Marcia's credentials include more than ten years experience in executive management and significant background in research, strategic planning, leadership development and business administration. She spent many years as a healthcare executive and holds a master's degree in business (MBA), a bachelor's degree in nursing (BSN) and undergraduate studies in anthropology. Today, Marcia is founder and principle of Beyond Zebra, a visionary consulting firm that strategically prepares people for a new life heading our way.

An internationally successful author, futurist and sought after speaker, Marcia builds bridges between science and mysticism as she explains how consciousness and our quantum universe work together to create our reality. By combining her medical, scientific and intuitive knowledge, she brings a fresh perspective to explain the world that lies behind our conventional reality curtain and reveals how people can access it for success. Her approach, while thoroughly grounded, is unique and beyond leading edge.

Schafer offers programs to help people learn how to think innovatively and prepare for the challenges of the coming years. Her clients come from all walks of life and all over the world to work with her. She is available for consulting, seminars and keynote presentations. Marcia can be reached through the www.beyondzebra.com website and by mail at:

Beyond Zebra
PMB D22
1334 E Chandler Blvd #5
Phoenix AZ 85048
Tel:480-460-7807/Fax: 480-460-7809
info@beyondzebra.com
www.beyondzebra.com

ORDER FORM

(SAN 299-7592)

Tel. orders: 480.460.7807
Fax orders: 480.460.7809
Internet orders: www.beyondzebra.com
info@beyondzebra.com

Postal Orders: Cosmic Destiny Press
PMB D22
1334 E. Chandler Blvd, Suite 5
Phoenix, AZ 85048

Confessions Of An Intergalactic Anthropologist

by Marcia Schafer

(ISBN 0-9668620-2-3)

Please send me ____ copies of *Confessions of an Intergalactic Anthropologist* at $19.95 each.

Ship to:

Name______________________________

Address______________________________

City______________State__________Zip______________

Phone______________Fax______________

E-mail Address______________________________

Shipping and handling: Inside U.S., add $5.00 for first book, $3.50 each book thereafter.
International orders contact us for current rates.

Sales Tax: Add $1.61 tax for **each** book shipped to Arizona addresses.

Payment (US Funds Only)

Check or Money Order ________
Credit Card ________

❑ VISA ❑ MasterCard ❑ American Express

Card Number:______________________________

Name on Card: ______________Expiration Date:__________

Signature:______________________________

Price ($19.95 each) $__________

Shipping ($5.00 first book, $3.50 thereafter) $__________

Applic. Tax ($1.61 per book) $__________

Total $__________

ORDER FORM

(SAN 299-7592)

Tel. orders: 480.460.7807
Fax orders: 480.460.7809
Internet orders: www.beyondzebra.com
info@beyondzebra.com

Postal Orders: Cosmic Destiny Press
PMB D22
1334 E. Chandler Blvd, Suite 5
Phoenix, AZ 85048

CONFESSIONS OF AN INTERGALACTIC ANTHROPOLOGIST

by Marcia Schafer

(ISBN 0-9668620-2-3)

Please send me ____ copies of *Confessions of an Intergalactic Anthropologist* at $19.95 each.

Ship to:

Name____

Address____

City__________________State__________Zip__________________

Phone______________________Fax______________________

E-mail Address____

Shipping and handling: Inside U.S., add $5.00 for first book, $3.50 each book thereafter.
International orders contact us for current rates.

Sales Tax: Add $1.61 tax for **each** book shipped to Arizona addresses.

Payment (US Funds Only)

Check or Money Order ______
Credit Card ______

❑ VISA ❑ MasterCard ❑ American Express

Card Number:____

Name on Card: ______________________Expiration Date:__________

Signature:____

Price ($19.95 each) $__________

Shipping ($5.00 first book, $3.50 thereafter) $__________

Applic. Tax ($1.61 per book) $__________

Total $__________

ORDER FORM

(SAN 299-7592)

Tel. orders:	480.460.7807	**Postal Orders:**	Cosmic Destiny Press
Fax orders:	480.460.7809		PMB D22
Internet orders:	www.beyondzebra.com		1334 E. Chandler Blvd, Suite 5
	info@beyondzebra.com		Phoenix, AZ 85048

Confessions Of An Intergalactic Anthropologist

by Marcia Schafer

(ISBN 0-9668620-2-3)

Please send me ____ copies of *Confessions of an Intergalactic Anthropologist* at $19.95 each.

Ship to:

Name______________________________

Address______________________________

City______________State________Zip____________

Phone______________Fax______________

E-mail Address______________________________

Shipping and handling: Inside U.S., add $5.00 for first book, $3.50 each book thereafter.
International orders contact us for current rates.

Sales Tax: Add $1.61 tax for **each** book shipped to Arizona addresses.

Payment (US Funds Only)

Check or Money Order ________
Credit Card ________

❑ VISA ❑ MasterCard ❑ American Express

Card Number:______________________________

Name on Card: ______________Expiration Date:__________

Signature:______________________________

Price ($19.95 each)	$__________
Shipping ($5.00 first book, $3.50 thereafter)	$__________
Applic. Tax ($1.61 per book)	$__________
Total	$__________

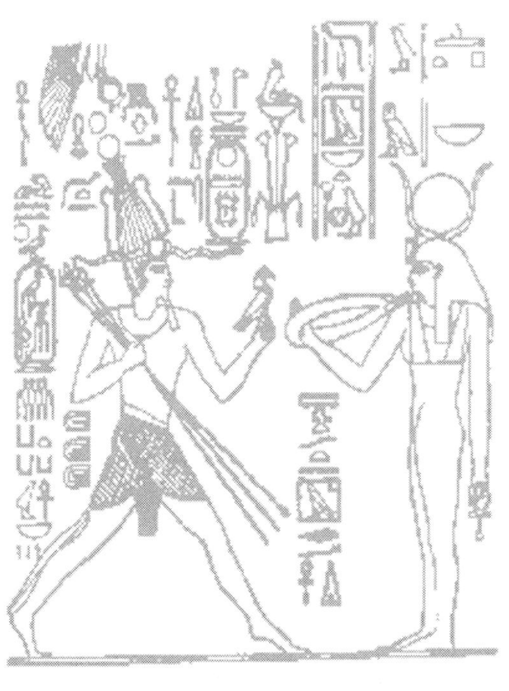